ALL OF ME
The True Story of a London Rose

Rose Neighbour was born on the wrong side of Acton, West London; her home had no bath and her mother worked in a steam laundry for threepence an hour. But Rose always dreamed of something better. *All of Me* follows her life through the twenties when she was a film extra and a chorus girl; the Depression of the thirties when 'Buddy can you spare a dime' was top of the pops and she sold song sheets in a market hall; the forties when she fell in love with a G.I. and the fifties when she worked for the BBC and met all the stars of Radio. *All of Me* is a nostalgic picture of London seen through the eyes of Rose, an indomitable spirit who has faced life with courage, joy and, above all, humour.

ALL OF ME

The True Story
of a London Rose

Rose Neighbour
as told to
Muriel Burgess

A Lythway Book

CHIVERS PRESS
BATH

First published 1979
by
W. H. Allen
This Large Print edition published by
Chivers Press
by arrangement with
Muriel Burgess
1989

ISBN 0 7451 1038 X

British Library Cataloguing in Publication Data

Neighbour, Rose
  All of me: the true story of a London Rose.—
  (Lythway large print)
  1. London. Neighbour, Rose. Autobiographies
  I. Title II. Burgess, Muriel
  942.1082'0924

  ISBN 0–7451–1038–X

For my mother, with love,
and for Thora Hird, who
made me do it

CONTENTS

1 What the fortune teller told me   1
2 I was born in Soap Suds Island   8
3 Friday night was Talent Night at
      the Globe   34
4 Those golden summers when I was
      young   55
5 I sold romance at sixpence a time   74
6 There must be more to marriage
      than misery   100
7 My love wore an American uniform   127
8 Picking up the pieces   153
9 Tea and sympathy at the BBC   175
10 Feeling at home in America   200
11 Put my pension in the post   216
12 There's no business like television   235
13 On location with a pack of wolves   253
14 Happy Christmas to all 'my artistes'   277

ALL OF ME
The True Story of a London Rose

CHAPTER ONE

WHAT THE FORTUNE TELLER
TOLD ME

I slammed shut the front door of my flat. Holding my ten-year-old son by the hand and with just two shillings in my purse, I walked out of my marriage. I must admit that my heart thumped as I went down the stairs, I had a moment of sheer panic, but the marriage that had started so well twelve years ago when I was nineteen, was now destroying me. 'You're on your own, Rose,' I told myself, 'and you've got to make it work.'

When we got to the bus stop, Brian, my son, said, 'Where we going, Mum?' He knew that something unusual had happened.

'Over to your Nan's.'

'When we coming back?'

Never, I thought to myself. But as the 607 made its slow way from Southall to Acton I began to feel more tense with apprehension. What was I going to do? To begin with there was no room for me at my mother's house. I knew she'd take Brian, he often spent a night over there, but how was I going to explain what had happened? In the year nineteen hundred and forty-four a woman was expected to make

1

the best of a bad bargain. To leave my husband and try to bring up my child alone was something my parents wouldn't understand.

I won't tell them, I decided. I'll get a job and a place to live first. But how was I going to do that? The two shillings in my purse wouldn't go far, and here was the bus conductor coming up for his fare.

1944 with the doodle-bugs and rockets raining down on London wasn't the best time to make a fresh start. I left Brian with my mother and father saying that I was going out for the evening and would pick him up next day. As I walked away I was glad I hadn't burdened them with my problem, and I remembered there was a place where I could spend the night.

I arrived at Piccadilly Circus at exactly the right time. The last train had just gone through and it was bedtime for the Londoners who preferred to sleep underground rather than risk the rockets overhead. The bedding rolls and the sleeping bags were being laid out and the picnic suppers being eaten. I trod carefully over the recumbent bodies looking for a place to sit.

A woman with two children on the only empty bench smiled at me as I approached. 'Come down for the night, have you?' I nodded. She moved up. 'There's room here.' She looked me over. 'Haven't you got anything with you?'

'No!' I could hardly explain that the last thing on my mind when I'd left home was to spend the night underground.

'It gets perishing cold sometimes. You'll freeze.'

'It doesn't matter.' I was fast reaching the stage where nothing mattered any more.

'Here! We've got a blanket to spare. Wrap yourself up in this.' My new friend and her children curled up and went to sleep. Everyone seemed to sleep. I sat there staring straight ahead and feeling very alone. Of course I didn't sleep a wink. I went over and over in my head what I must do. First, find a job. I hadn't been trained to do anything in particular. I could do invisible mending. I could tint photographs with life-like colour. I could play the piano and tap dance, but whether they'd be much help I didn't know. Then I remembered all the big cinemas around Leicester Square. It didn't take much know-how to be an usherette. Any fool could switch on a torch.

At seven next morning I was in one of the special washrooms set up for the emergency, trying to smarten myself up. I must have succeeded for the manager of the first cinema I visited, the Empire, Leicester Square, gave me a job as usherette.

Everything was much better in the daylight. I telephoned a friend and she said, 'Lilian can have you. Her husband's away in the Forces, she's expecting a baby, and she's got a six-room house in Harrow.' Then I went back to Acton

3

and explained what had happened to my mother and father. It wasn't as bad as I'd expected. As always they stood by me and said that Brian must remain with them for the time being.

The Empire, Leicester Square was a lovely cinema, one of the biggest in London; there were a thousand seats downstairs. Watching people enjoy themselves did lift my spirits. We worked two shifts, one that started in the morning and the other that ended at ten at night. Cinemas closed early during the war so that the patrons and staff could catch the last tube train home.

I made friends with one of the other usherettes, a pretty curly-haired girl called Doris. She was shy and quiet, the exact opposite to me who had always been a chatterbox. But like me, she had her problems. One of them was her love affair with the film projectionist at the cinema next door.

'Do you think I ought to marry him?' she kept asking.

'Forget it,' I told her. 'Look what happened to me.'

One afternoon she asked if I'd go down with her to the East End. She'd heard of a fortune teller who lived in the Mile End Road. 'She's got a great reputation,' she declared, 'so if she tells me I ought to marry him, I will.'

'Fortune telling's a load of old rubbish,' I said. 'You don't really believe in it, do you?'

I saw that I'd hurt her feelings, so I agreed that when we were both on early shift we'd go down to the East End together. What with the doodle-bugs and the black-out, a journey to an unknown part of London was quite frightening.

When we got out of the tube station at Mile End, not only had the complete darkness of the black-out descended, but we'd hardly gone a hundred yards when an air raid warning sounded. There wasn't a soul about.

'Let's go back,' I pleaded. 'There must be a fortune teller nearer home.'

Doris, for a shy quiet girl, was very determined. 'She's famous,' she cried. 'People come from miles around to see her.'

We found the place where she lived eventually. One of those old-fashioned Peabody Buildings that used to teem with families of East Enders. Part of it looked as if it had been demolished by bombs, just the middle section was still standing, and even that looked derelict.

With the aid of our flickering torches we started to climb the stone steps. On each landing we paused for breath and there wasn't a sign of life. On the fourth floor, where she was supposed to live, we banged on doors until at last a chink of light showed and we knew we'd found the last remaining inhabitant.

To me the fortune teller was an instant disappointment. I'd expected someone with flashing gypsy eyes and gold earrings; the woman who let us in looked like any other East End cockney. She wore a floral pinafore and carpet slippers, and the first thing she did was make us a nice cup of tea. Her little flat was warm and welcoming and with the black-out curtains in place again, we forgot the rockets outside.

Doris went over and sat with her at the table covered with a brown chenille cloth. They went through a long rigmarole of cutting cards, oohing and aahing when a particularly significant card turned up. I could see that Doris was enjoying herself and I suppose with marriage being such a lottery, it was as good a way as any of choosing a husband.

'He's the one for you, me gel,' the fortune teller said at last. 'The cards never lie to me.' Doris paid the requisite five bob and the fortune teller turned to me. 'You next, gel.'

'No thanks,' I said firmly, 'cards have never brought me luck.' I didn't tell her that the husband I'd just left was a compulsive gambler who'd lost every penny we had on the horses and the dogs. There was another quite compelling reason for not wanting my fortune told. I had no money.

'Come on,' she said, as if she could read my mind. 'I'll do it for nothing.'

She made me cut the cards and straight away I learned that I'd had a lot of trouble. I didn't need to come down to the Mile End Road to find that out. Then she said, 'There's a long journey here, at least three thousand miles. And then there's another one, and another.' I cut the cards again. She looked at me with surprise. 'You've got some very important and famous people coming into your life.'

I smiled. My mother's house in Acton had an outside toilet and no bathroom. My family had been poor all their lives. The only famous people I ever saw were the film stars in the posters at the Empire, Leicester Square.

'You smile,' said the fortune teller, 'but that's where your destiny is gel, with all those famous people.'

'Not me.'

She wagged a finger. 'You'll go out of my door, you'll forget everything I've said to you. And then one fine day you'll remember my words. This will all come true, gel.'

And would you believe it. She was absolutely right. Years later I stood at the stern rail of the ship taking me to America. I gazed at the wake of the ship streaming out into the sunshine and I suddenly remembered the words of the fortune teller of the Mile End Road. Everything she said had come true.

CHAPTER TWO

I WAS BORN IN SOAP SUDS ISLAND

I was born in Soap Suds Island. That's what we called our part of Acton. Everywhere you looked there was a laundry with little clouds of steam eddying out of the back door, and there was a special smell in the air of yellow soap, chlorine and hot flat irons on damp linen. In those days the nobs of Mayfair never did their own washing. Everything was sent down to the Curzon, the Carlton, the Victoria, the Sunny Maid or Ford's Hand Laundry where my mother worked.

My mother started work in the Laundry when she was fourteen and rather like a miner who earned his living down the pits, she was determined that no child of hers was ever going to goffer a ruffle or hand press a pleat for two shillings a day in a laundry.

Elizabeth Boult, my mother, was a woman of character. When she told her father that she wanted to marry the boy next door he exploded. 'Marry a man who clears up dirty glasses in a pub! And apart from that, Lizzie, he's a Catholic.'

Lizzie said to her sweetheart, 'Could you find something a little bit better. Then I'll try him again.'

James Nestor, the boy next door loved the convivial atmosphere of the Anchor Pub in Acton High Street, where he worked. He wasn't a drinker but he enjoyed the laughter and the jokes, and the talk. James was easy going, being a potman at the Anchor suited him, but rather than lose Lizzie he found a boring job with the Gas Company.

'He's still a Catholic,' growled her father. Not that he had anything against James, but there were many layers of society in Petersfield Road where they lived. The Boults had a position to keep up. Mr Boult's father had been one of the first Bow Street Runners and he himself was now a builder, while the Nestors way back came from Ireland and being Catholic made them suspect.

Lizzie Boult and James Nestor were married on August Bank Holiday Monday, 1910, at All Saints Church, South Acton, and their wedding was a great big street affair. Everyone in Petersfield Road was invited. They had pins and kegs of beer, a ham, meat pies, jellies and trifles and a big wedding cake. Lizzie, who was small and brown haired, wore a white muslin dress with lace inserts and a high boned collar. All the Boult women were small and fair skinned and so are my sister and I.

The young couple settled down in the bottom half of one of the Victorian terraced houses, just

9

round the corner from their parents' home. No 38 Petersfield Road had once been red brick. Now it was black with London soot, but Lizzie's lace curtains at the window were always spotless. The colour of your curtains showed what kind of woman you were, she said.

Lizzie brought us up on her sayings. 'Hard work never hurt anyone.' 'God pays his debts without money.' 'There's no such word as can't.' She had been taught 'manners', and we were brought up the same way. Everyone was poor in Petersfield Road, but there were degrees of poverty. As long as her children had shoes to wear and enough food, Lizzie could hold her head up. I remember seeing children playing in the cobbled streets around us without shoes. That was the ultimate disgrace, the ultimate fear.

I was born in 1912 and my sister about 16 months later—just in time for my father to have a look at her before going off to war. He joined the Middlesex Regiment and was sent to Egypt. He stayed there for four years.

My mother was left with £1 a week to bring up her two children. She got in touch with Rose, her sister, the one I'd been named after, who lived in Battersea. Her husband Uncle Dick had joined up too and was with the army in France.

'Come and live with me, Rose,' she said. 'Give up your house in Battersea, and we'll share the rent of No 38.' The rent was about eight shillings a week.

Rose with her little girl Edna came to live with us. She liked the idea of being back with all her sisters and relations again.

'Rose,' said my mother, not long after—she was the one with the ideas—'they've turned the White City Exhibition into a munitions factory. Women are earning good money down there. Now if you worked there during the day, I could look after the three children, then I'll work there at night and you'll be home with the children. We can switch the shifts as we please.'

It worked very well. The White City was not far from where we lived. Acton, in fact was a good centre for everything. There was Shepherd's Bush and Hammersmith down the Goldhawk Road. Then on the West Side there were posh districts of Ealing and Chiswick down by the river. We were poor in our part of Acton, but it wasn't the grinding poverty of the sweat shops of the East End.

Every Saturday night the two young women had a party. Very respectable, just sisters and uncles and aunts, and if Uncle Dick was home on leave from France he'd bring some of his Tommy friends. I loved Uncle Dick. He was a dark handsome young man, and he was a Catholic. I don't know how the Boults, strict Protestants, managed to get two Catholics as sons-in-law.

11

Of course we hadn't got a piano, only the rich had pianos. But one of the uncles could play the mouth organ. Aunt Rose would stand in the middle of our front room, with the three piece leather suite and the aspidistra on the table under the window and sing. She had a lovely soprano voice. The brass bed where we three little girls slept would be pushed into a corner and covered with a tablecloth and cushions.

Aunt Rose's favourite song was, 'God bring him back to me, over the mighty sea . . .' The English Channel took on the proportions of a mighty ocean and a tear would roll down my cheek as I thought of Uncle Dick. Then everyone would cheer up and sing the war songs, 'It's a long way to Tipperary' and 'Pack up your Troubles'. One night before I was sent off to bed in my mother's bedroom, I sang a song, 'Keep the Homes Fires Burning'. I loved the applause. It was my first taste of performing in public.

Towards the end of the war Aunt Rose went down to Folkestone to meet the cross channel ferry that was bringing Uncle Dick home on leave. When they came back to Petersfield Road, Aunt Rose said, 'Lizzie, we've got to take the girls to the barber to get their hair cut in the latest French style.' She'd seen a very smart Frenchwoman coming ashore with her little girl. The child's black shining hair was bobbed with a fringe.

My father's barber, Mr Brown, performed the bobbing under Aunt Rose's instructions. One by one we sat in his high chair with a sheet tucked round our necks. It was a special favour for my absent father.

My new hairstyle was the first thing my father noticed when he came home in 1918. He couldn't get over how much I'd changed, from the little two-year-old to this grown girl of six. I climbed onto his lap, put my arms round his neck and kissed him soundly. He called me 'My little Rose'. It was the beginning of a deep mutual love that lasted until the day he died.

Grace hid behind a chair and cried every time the strange man came near her. My mother did say, 'What's that thing you've grown. We'll get that moustache shaved off first thing.'

I remember that I sat contentedly on my father's knee all evening and eventually I went to sleep still hearing his voice telling my mother of all the strange things he had seen and done. He'd been away for four years in Egypt and the Near East, and he had a long tale to tell. All through my childhood he enthralled us with his tales of the Orient. He was one of the lucky ones. His four years in the army had changed him, opened new horizons, educated him, made him look at life with fresh insight.

The Padre of his regiment had taken an interest in him. He'd introduced him to reading, lent him books, discussed them with

13

him. For the first time in his life young James Nestor had an opportunity to learn and discover the world about him. He travelled, he went to Jerusalem and saw the holy places, and yet, for all that, when he came home, he had no religion, he had become an atheist.

He learned to box, he became interested in sport. He joined the regimental band and learned to play the cornet. His new appreciation of music made him say to my mother, 'Lizzie, one day we'll buy a piano, and the girls shall be taught to play.'

★   ★   ★

The flags came down, the husbands were home from the war and 1919 turned out to be a terrible year for us. There were no jobs for the heroes. The factories that had boomed during the war closed down. Bullets and khaki uniforms were out of fashion.

My father couldn't find a job. Unemployment became a terrible spectre that stayed with my family for years. The rent had to be paid or you were out on the street with your bits and pieces. And there was the shame of it all, with the neighbours watching behind their lace curtains. My mother and father had never had much, but they clung to their pride. Fair enough, in those days, everyone in Petersfield Road helped everyone else, but to be the object of pity was unbearable. Only the family, the brothers and sisters, the mothers and fathers, were ever told when there wasn't a penny piece in the house.

Not everyone in Petersfield Road was so hard up. The woman in the flat over us bought a gramophone with a horn, and we could hear the strains of her new music, but then her husband hadn't gone away to war. He was one of those who'd stayed at home and had a good job.

My father wasn't bitter. There were too many other men like him. Uncle Dick over at Battersea was out of work, and so were my two uncles in Acton. The money my mother had saved during her years on munitions was quickly used up; the hand-out for the unemployed ex-soldiers was a pittance. There was only one thing she could do, she went back to work at Ford's Hand Laundry. She was a first class ironer. The nobs in Mayfair still had their monogrammed linen sheets laundered, the ruffles round their embroidered pillowcases still had to be goffered by hand. She worked from eight in the morning until eight at night for 2/3d (12p) with an extra threepence if she stayed until nine o'clock.

I've seen pictures of the unemployed after the 1918 war, lines of grey looking men in cloth caps and mufflers shuffling towards the head of the queue at the Labour Exchange. My father must have been one of them. Lloyd George had

15

brought in an Unemployment Insurance Bill in 1911, but it wasn't until 1919 that 'dole' was handed out. It was a charitable gift and was small and very selectively applied. I remember that my father eventually had to go to the Board of Guardians to plead his case. The Board of Guardians were in charge of the workhouses and to end up in a workhouse that was the biggest fear of all.

Because she had a job, my mother was spared from going to the pawnshop, but she lent all her little pieces of jewellery to her sisters to take down to the pawnshop when things were tough. She had a little gold watch bought in the palmy days of the war and the engagement ring my father had given her. They were her two standbys that would always raise a few shillings. The charges of the pawnshop were, I believe, a halfpenny on every two shillings and sixpence borrowed, per month. It didn't sound much but it added up. In and out went her treasures. Some of them stayed in forever never to be redeemed, but the gold watch was saved and one day given to me.

West's, the corner grocery store, did give 'tick'. You could buy groceries on account and pay at the end of the week, but my mother tried to pay as she went along. Look what had happened to poor Aunt Rose.

Uncle Dick over in Battersea was out of work and Aunt Rose had just had a baby, another little girl. One day she hadn't a penny in her purse, the baby was ailing and cried for food, so Aunt Rose put her pride in her pocket and went along to the corner shop to ask if she could have a tin of Nestle's milk on tick.

The owner of the shop said, 'Sorry ducks. No tick, too many people are out of work. I'd never get my money if I let all of you lot pay me when you can.'

If she'd had the strength Aunt Rose would have walked across Battersea Bridge to Acton and her family. But Acton was six miles away. In the end she found a neighbour who lent her the money to buy a tin of milk.

The baby died soon after. True, she was an ailing little girl, but I think those bleak years after the war marked my family. I grew up with a tiny core of resentment fed by the stories I heard over the years of the bad times.

And yet, although we were living on the edge of disaster, and poverty in varying degrees was all around us, I didn't realise just how poor we were. My sister Grace and I were kept clean and tidy. We always seemed to have enough to eat. Even the affair of the charity boots hurt my parents more than it hurt me.

Our shoes were worn out, there were holes in the soles and in the wet weather, the rain came through the cardboard linings. One morning my mother produced two pairs of black leather lace-up boots. They were heavy with sturdy

17

uppers and with steel Blakeys on the heels and toes.

'I don't like them,' I complained. 'Why do we have to wear them, Mum?'

'They're good strong boots. They'll keep your feet dry.'

Grace snivelled a bit and said that the rough leather chafed her ankles.

'You'll soon get used to them. Now be good girls and get ready for school. I'll be here at dinner time.' She kissed us goodbye and left for her ten minute walk to the Laundry over in Avenue Road. She was always home when we got back at twelve, waiting for us with a hot meal.

'Heh! Have you seen Rosie Nestor's boots? Her Mum's got 'em free from the Parish. Ooh, don't they look 'orrible.' Some of the children at school taunted us. Children are like that—even the nicest ones. A lot of them wore charity boots but it pleased them to be able to get their own back on the Nestor girls. Grace was still snivelling on and off when we went home at dinner time. As soon as she saw Mum she burst into loud sobs. 'I hate these boots,' she wept. 'I'm never going back to school no more.'

My mother looked at them. 'What happened?'

'They said you got them from the Parish. They're . . . you know . . . free boots.' My

18

lower lip trembled. 'I don't want to wear Parish boots, Mum.'

My father who had just come in for his dinner stood in the scullery listening to us. His face tightened. He refused to sit down and eat his food. Blind anger made him pull on his cap again and shout. 'I'm off out, Lizzie, and I won't be back till I've got the money to buy the girls some shoes.'

He came back that afternoon with a job. The first job he'd got since he left the army. It wasn't a very good job, he was to work as a labourer shovelling coke at a small engineering factory called Berwick's. It didn't last very long either, for the factory closed down soon after. But it was a job. My father felt a man again, he had work and he could keep his children in shoes.

★   ★   ★

On the wall of our living room hung a photograph of Aunt Agnes. A round black and white picture in a thin gilt frame. Aunt Agnes, the middle one of my mother's five sisters, was pictured as a serious-faced girl of about twenty, with straight hair pulled back and anxious eyes that perpetually scanned our faces as we ate our mid-day dinner.

With monotonous regularity I asked, 'What happened to Aunt Agnes, Mum?'

'She left one night and never came back,' said

my mother doling out the Brussels sprouts.

'Didn't she leave a note? Didn't she say goodbye?'

'No,' said my mother, 'she just left. Now eat your dinner and stop asking questions.'

The disappearance of Aunt Agnes fascinated me, but no matter how much I pleaded, nothing more than, 'She left one night and never came back', was forthcoming. This seeming indifference to Aunt Agnes's whereabouts mystified me. The Boults were a closely-knit family, what had she done to be so disowned? Had she committed a crime? Had it been that terrible misdemeanour, 'getting herself into trouble'? Where are you Aunt Agnes, I used to wonder, as I ate my boiled potatoes. Are you living in some far off country?

Looking back I can see that Aunt Agnes had not been completely rejected. Her photograph hung in our living room. As long as our wistful Aunt was up there, home was always home. The iron kettle still hummed on the hob of the big black range; the red enamel tea caddy, a wedding present, still had pride of place on the mantelpiece.

★　　★　　★

Most of my father's sisters lived in Acton too. Aunts Lizzie, Nell, Ada and Florrie had all married and left home, but Aunt Daisy the youngest and the apple of her mother's eye was still living at home. Granny Nestor, a lady with a strong personality, was determined that Daisy would stay with her and be a comfort in her old age. As Daisy was very pretty and full of life the rest of the family watched the situation with interest.

The Wembley Exhibition in 1924 was the greatest thing that had happened for years. All the might of the great British Empire was there for us to see, all the peoples of the Empire upon which the sun never sets were there in their native dress. It was wonderful to be British in 1924. I knew perfectly well that as long as I could wrap myself up in a Union Jack no wicked foreigner could ever harm me—at least not unless he wanted our gun boats at his backdoor.

Aunt Daisy found a job at Wembley Exhibition as a programme seller and very soon she caught the eye of one of the cowboys in the Rodeo show. It was love at first sight for Daisy and Wild Bill Clarke. When Granny Nestor was given the news that they intended to get married and live in America, she took to her bed with grief.

Daisy and Wild Bill were married at Isleworth with quite a bit of publicity, Bill wearing his ten-gallon hat and full cowboy rig tossed a lassoo round Daisy's neck while a press photographer took their pictures. Afterwards, the blissful newlyweds toured England and Scotland with the rodeo show. I was so proud to have a real live cowboy in the family.

When the time came for Daisy and Bill to catch the ship to America Granny Nestor collapsed with a mysterious illness and was said to be at death's door. She implored Daisy to stay with her until the end.

'There's nothing wrong with her,' said my mother shrewdly. She herself had survived years of living with her domineering mother-in-law round the corner. 'As soon as Bill's on the ship, Granny'll be out of bed like a jack-in-the-box.'

Unfortunately as soon as Granny Nestor was on her feet again, Daisy was rushed to hospital to have an emergency operation. 'The poor girl had tubes sticking out all over her,' said Granny contentedly, 'she won't be able to go to America for months.'

Wild Bill Clarke kept sending the boat fare, Aunt Daisy kept packing her suitcase, but at the last moment Granny Nestor always found a way to stop her going. However one day Granny Nestor took to her bed once too often. In the middle of a nervous collapse when Daisy's thoughts were turning towards America, Granny met her Maker.

At the funeral my mother was heard to remark sagely, 'God pays his debts without money.'

Daisy was free at last. She sent a telegram to Wild Bill, '*Mother died last month. Longing to see you*'. Daisy waited, the weeks became months but not a word from Wild Bill. Her letters were returned 'Gone Away'. In desperation Daisy asked the American Salvation Army to find her cowboy husband, but he had disappeared. I was sure that Wild Bill had died a true cowboy's death in those wide open ranges of the Far West.

After a long time even Daisy had to accept that Wild Bill had headed for the Last Round-up. When she was legally made a widow she married again. She had two daughters and one of them sent me a newspaper cutting the other day. A local newspaper was running a 'Where are they now' feature and someone had dug up the old wedding picture of Wild Bill and Daisy from the archives. Unfortunately the two star-crossed lovers were both dead by then and Granny Nestor may well have sighed as she turned once more in her grave.

$$\star \qquad \star \qquad \star$$

We were going through one of the good periods. My father had a job as steward at the British Legion Club. He ran the small clubhouse where ex-soldiers used to come to drink and yarn. They played billiards or cards and talked about the lot of the working man over a glass of beer. 'The Club' was the haven for many an ex-serviceman, and my father ran the Acton branch well; keeping the accounts, ordering the beer, organising a special evening on Saturdays when wives and children were allowed in. It was the kind of work he enjoyed, in the convivial atmosphere of men off duty, relaxed and happy.

My mother had been promoted at the Laundry. She was now a forewoman in charge of the giant Calendars, the big rollers that pressed, in clouds of steam, the sheets and tablecloths. No longer did she spend hours over a gas jet heating the goffering irons. But she still used them at home. They looked like curling tongs and with a twist of the wrist she used to take them round the flounced edge of a petticoat or the frills of a muslin blouse.

Over in Battersea Uncle Dick had found a job at the local brewery, so they were solvent once more. On Saturday nights he, with Aunt Rose and Edna, used to come over to Acton for the concert at the British Legion Club. We children were allowed to sit in the backroom with a glass of fizzy lemonade and we would cluster in the doorway to listen to the sing-song and watch the paid entertainer who often did a clog dance. One evening they had a stand-up comedian, he was considered vulgar and was never invited

24

back, but one of his jokes stuck in my head. I tried it on the assembled children and they rocked with laughter. I couldn't understand what it meant and neither could they, but it sounded too funny for words.

The following Saturday evening, I was once more regaling the kiddiwinkies with my story—I was getting a reputation as a real comic—when my father put his head round the door, to see that we children were behaving ourselves.

'Dad,' I called, the excitement going straight to my head.

'What's the difference between an actress getting out of her bath and a bishop?'

'What's that?' said my father warily.

'The bishop has a soul full of hope and the actress has a hole full of soap.' I doubled up with laughter, I laughed and I laughed until I realised that the room had become strangely silent. My father's face was a picture.

'Lizzie,' he roared. My mother came hurrying over. 'Take Rose home,' he shouted. 'She's been very rude.'

Rude, what was rude about my little joke, I asked my mother as she trundled me back home? Everyone laughed when I told it, so it must be funny.

'Never you mind,' admonished my mother, 'You'll have to learn to watch your tongue, Rose, my girl, or it'll get you into trouble.' I never did learn unfortunately, my tongue has always run away with me.

*   *   *

My father was strict with us and so was my mother. By the time we were ten, both Grace and I had been taught to run the home. My mother was out at work, and we were expected to make the beds, clean the grates, do the shopping and prepare the tea for Dad when he came home at five. Two fresh herrings with soft roes was one of our favourites, the herrings for our parents and the soft roes for us. We had little in the way of material possessions, but the greatest gift children can have: two parents who loved each other and loved us. We were a very happy, united family.

On Saturday afternoons my mother dressed us up in the new sports rig, white blouses and shorts, and we went running with my father round Acton Park. He was a great man for sport and loved cross-country running. Sometimes he'd take us up to Parliament Hill Fields in Hampstead to watch the Finchley Harriers. On Sundays we wore our best, shantung silk frocks and side buttoned boots. Everyone in Petersfield Road dressed up in their best on Sunday. This was the day we made our weekly pilgrimage calling on all the aunts and uncles and the four grandparents who lived next door to each other.

'How's your Dad?' would ask Granny Nestor grimly, inferring that his lot was a hard one.

'How's your Mum?' would ask Grandma Boult, just as partisan. And then we'd get a halfpenny to spend at Mrs Bassett's the sweet shop.

Our happy life was disrupted one quiet evening. My mother had the sewing machine on the table. She was teaching me how to cut out and make a blouse when the back door opened into the scullery and Aunt Rose walked in. As soon as we saw her we knew that something was terribly wrong. Aunt Rose, who always followed the fashion, wasn't wearing a hat. In those days a woman never went out calling without a hat. And Aunt Rose's coat was wrongly buttoned as if she'd dragged it on hardly knowing what she was doing.

'It's Dick,' whispered my Aunt. 'He's in Lambeth Hospital and they're not sure if he's going to live.'

As my mother led Aunt Rose to a seat by the fire, her eyes sought out mine. 'Get the table cleared off, Rose.'

While I moved the machine, the brown paper patterns, the pins and the poplin cloth, I listened intently. I was learning about life by listening. I didn't always understand the women's talk, but it was completely enthralling.

'He's got blisters the size of saucers all over his chest and shoulders. Even if he gets over it,

27

he'll never be able to work again.' The enormity of the tragedy suddenly seemed to render her silent. She sat staring at my mother.

'Make some tea, Rose,' ordered my mother, and then run down to Aunt Alice and ask if she's got any brandy in the house. Just an egg cup full.'

I hated missing the drama and I was down the street and back again carrying half a wine-glassful of brandy before Aunt Alice had had time to take off her apron and follow me. I hadn't really missed much, as soon as Aunt Alice arrived the terrible story was told again.

Uncle Dick's job at the brewery concerned brewing the beer in giant wooden and copper vats. Around each vat was constructed a wooden platform which Uncle Dick would mount to stir the ingredients with a large ladle. In one of the vats a mixture was being brought to the boil, Uncle Dick got up to stir the contents, his foot slipped on a wet greasy patch and over he went tumbling into the scalding liquid. Only the prompt action of another worker who dragged him out saved him from being killed instantly.

Aunt Rose sipped her brandy and the three sisters sat together shaking their heads and sighing as they talked of the bleak future that loomed ahead. 'We were just getting straight,' said Aunt Rose bitterly her face taut and white. 'We were going down to Hastings on a trip for the day next Easter Monday. I'd made a new dress for Edna.'

Even my mother couldn't find the heart to quote one of her famous sayings to comfort poor Aunt Rose. The whole family were just getting over the lean years after the war and she hadn't forgotten what happened when there was no money coming in.

Long after Aunt Rose had been put on the tram to go home to Battersea, my mother and father discussed her problem. Even if Uncle Dick recovered, they agreed, he'd be a hopeless invalid, disfigured, a shell of a man. 'We'll have to help them out, Lizzie,' my father said.

My mother sighed. All the good things she was at last experiencing, the new carpet she planned to buy for the front room, the red serge dresses for us, even the dividend she got when she shopped at the Co-op shop, were all evaporating into thin air. The only thing left was one of her sayings: 'Earth has no sorrow heaven cannot heal,' she quoted, and we all hoped fervently that this time she was right.

Two days later, Aunt Rose was round to see us again. A very different woman this time. She had been to the hospital and seen Uncle Dick, even spoke to him and he'd replied through the bandages. He was going to get better. It would be a long job, but he would recover.

'And Lizzie,' she told me mother, 'guess who came to see me yesterday. Mr Briggs!'

Mr Briggs was the manager of the brewery, one of the high-ups who always wore a bowler hat and a bow tie. 'The brewery are going to pay me Dick's wages every week, all the time he is in hospital. Not a penny less.'

My mother smiled for the first time in two days. Suddenly she was reprieved, the new carpet for the front room swam back in front of her eyes. 'But what about when he comes out?' she asked cautiously, before she accepted her good fortune.

'Dick is going to have a pension for the rest of his life,' Aunt Rose announced proudly. 'Mr Briggs said, "I want to take all the worries off your shoulders. You nurse your husband back to health and the brewery will look after him and his family for the rest of his life."'

'For ever?' said my mother faintly. 'Oh, my goodness.'

'You see,' I said to Grace. 'Happy ever after. It's just like a storybook.'

And in a way it was. Uncle Dick and Aunt Rose's fortunes were changed by his accident. It was a long time before he was well again, but Aunt Rose nursed him faithfully, the burns healed and he wasn't even scarred. He didn't go back to the brewery, but his pension was still paid to him and he was able to start a business on his own. He became a window cleaner. They moved up in the world. They were better off than they had ever been. Edna had a dolls' house for Christmas and they were the first people I knew to buy a crystal wireless set. We used to go round to see them and sit with the earphones on, each child was allotted ten minutes' listening-in time.

★　　　★　　　★

One of the high spots of our week was the late night show on Saturday night. Grace and I would sit up in our brass bedstead in the front room, part the curtains just enough to get a view of the pavement outside, lit by the soft yellow glow of the gas lamp, and listen for the first raucous strains of 'Mother Kelly's Doorstep' to come floating down Petersfield Road. It was throwing out time at the Elephant and Castle, the Six Bells and the King's Head. The Saturday night fights were about to begin.

Priory Road School was on the opposite side of the road, and next to it, in a little corner of its own, stood the Mortuary, a small, low brick building surrounded by iron railings. The Mortuary, to us, was just part of the scenery, the fact that it was a repository for dead bodies worried us not at all. The best fights took place outside the Mortuary.

Near us lived two feuding Irish families. The Kellys, staunch Catholics from Dublin, and the McKeuons, staunch Protestants from Belfast. Hardly a Saturday night went by without a

31

member of one family having a go at a member of the other. But even if they managed to get inside their respective front doors without violence, it was great entertainment just watching and listening to the verbal exchanges.

My parents had never been drinking people and rarely went inside the pubs that flourished on every street corner. Perhaps that was one of the reasons we stayed solvent, although, on the other hand, if you were poor and miserable, three penn'orth of gin must have been a comfort.

First past our windows came the happy drunks, singing their hearts out, arms round each other's shoulders. Anaesthetised, blissfully drunk, rolling perilously near the gutter, they recovered their balance just in time. One of the ladies lifted her skirts above her knees and danced a spirited jig. Grace and I smiled at each other, it was going to be a good night tonight.

I caught my breath, Mrs Kelly hove into view. She was a very fat lady who winter and summer wore a black straw boater pinned on her hair. Both her hands were clasped firmly round Mr Kelly's upper arm dragging him along. With the free arm he was shaking his fist at someone behind him and yelling 'Yer great black Prod! Come near me and I'll brain yer!'

Mrs Kelly gave him another yank homewards and then the unexpected happened. Mr Kelly aimed a sudden blow at his wife and knocked her right off her feet. Immediately the thin, bony figure of Mrs McKeuon appeared, 'Yer dirty bully,' she screamed at him. 'All you're good for's knocking bleeding women about.'

Surprisingly nimble for her bulk, Mrs Kelly sprang to her feet. 'Leave my husband alone, you cow.' She gave Mrs McKeuon a shove. And then, in front of our delighted eyes, the two ladies went for each other.

'Girls!' My father's voice made us dive under the bedclothes. He pulled the curtains together, blacking out the finale of the battle, although we could still hear the curses and screams outside. 'Don't let me catch you out of bed again.' Before he closed the door on us he said, 'Your mother and I have decided that we're going to buy a piano.'

'A piano!' Our heads appeared once more.

'And if you're good girls we'll send you to Professor Matthews to have lessons. Now go to sleep and dream about it.'

Darkness fell around us once more. The howls of Mrs Kelly and Mrs McKeuon faded into the night and all I could hear was the gentle breathing of the sleeping Grace. So I was to learn how to play the piano! I wasn't altogether pleased. I would much rather learn how to dance. Ever since I'd been to the pantomime my burning ambition was to become a chorus girl and wear salmon pink tights and a skirt with spangles. I knew instinctively that my father wouldn't approve. And yet, I crossed my fingers under the bedclothes. I'd work it somehow. I'd get onto the stage one day.

CHAPTER THREE

FRIDAY NIGHT WAS TALENT NIGHT AT THE GLOBE

I can't bear it, I thought to myself, I can't bear another Lake Windermere, a Dartmoor pony or a Cockington Forge.

'Rose,' said Mrs Allen severely, 'watch that stencil. I don't want it smudged.' Her nose, her left eye and the left side of her mouth suddenly twitched violently upwards. For eight hours of every day not only did I have the Lake District, Cockington Forge and the Isle of Skye to contend with, I also had Mrs Allen's twitch. It was all too much.

My father wanted me to go into business. He wanted me to be trained so that I could always earn a few bob, and perhaps one day I might open a little business of my own. He came home just before I left school at fourteen full of plans for my future. Someone at the British Legion Club had told him all about it.

'You're going to learn about colour photography,' he told me. 'You won't earn

34

much to begin with, seven shillings and sixpence a week, but you'll be a trained operator, apprenticed to a good trade.'

One Monday morning armed with a flask of tea and a packet of sandwiches for my lunch, I reported to Madame Allen's studio in Ealing Broadway. The studio turned out to be a room in Mrs Allen's flat over a greengrocer's shop. There wasn't a camera in sight just a long wooden table and around it sat four other young girls, seven and sixpenny apprentices, like myself. Madame Allen sat at the top of the table sucking her teeth and twitching. Poor woman, she was very plain and she had this nervous affliction, but there was nothing wrong with her business acumen. Apprentices came and apprentices went but her colour photographs went on forever. They're probably still on the top shelf of some village post office in the Outer Hebrides.

Every postcard picturing a sylvan scene such as the Fairy Glen in the Isle of Man, had its own set of stencils. The first stencil was placed over the black and white picture and the paintwork began. A dab of blue for the sky, another stencil, and a blob of white for the cloud, then another for the green grass, brown for the trees, and a snitch of yellow for the buttercups.

'You do it like this, Rose,' said Mrs Allen that first morning, giving me the only lesson of

35

my apprenticeship. She wagged the paintbrush at me and twitched, 'Whatever you do, don't smudge the paint on the stencil or you'll spoil the next postcard.'

'It's like being locked up in a prison workroom,' I told my father. 'We sit round this table all day painting picture after picture and Mrs Allen watches every move we make. No one's allowed to talk.'

'But you're learning a trade.'

'I've learnt it Dad. I know all there is to know about tinting pictures by hand. There's no future in it. In America they are doing it with a camera.' I hesitated. 'My friend Peggy Henderson says there's a job going at Eastman's.'

'You don't want any old job, Rose.'

'I shall be learning a trade, Dad. If I go to Eastman's they'll send me to their school to learn all about invisible mending, and furthermore,' I played my trump card, 'they'll pay me ten shillings a week.'

Eastman's in Acton Vale was a dyeing and cleaning factory. On Tuesday of every week I was sent up to the school in Tottenham Court Road and taught to mend silk stockings with a stylus needle picking up the dropped stitch and carrying it up through the ladder to be tied with a neat knot at the top. Silk stockings were expensive and it was worth paying out sixpence to have a ladder mended. Working girls, like

36

me, wore lisle or shiny aritifical silk.

After four lessons I was considered expert enough to go back to Eastman's where I sat in the Ladies' Hat Department mending silk stockings and sewing the trimmings back on the ladies' hats that came in to be cleaned and reblocked. It wasn't the most fascinating work in the world but working with a crowd of lively girls was heaven after Madame Allen's studio. At lunchtime someone would bring out the portable gramophone and we would dance round the workroom. Taller girls partnering the small ones in the waltz, the foxtrot and the tango.

On the day I started work at Madame Allen's studio, my mother gave up her job at Ford's Hand Laundry. She thought it only fair that she should be at home now to look after the two workers. My father had given up his job at the British Legion Club because of the late hours and was now a fitter with the Gas Company. I gave my mother all my wages and she handed me back pocket money. I was perfectly happy with this arrangement, and it went on until the day I left home to get married. By then my pocket money was up to two shillings and sixpence a week.

Soon after I was fifteen I gave up piano lessons with Professor Matthews. I was through to Smallwood's Tutors, I'd won five certificates from the College of Music and I was now playing what really interested me, popular music, syncopation. I was mad about popular music. For me everything was mixed up in the lyrics of songs, the beat of the dance. I was stage struck, and so were my best friends, Peggy Henderson and Winnie Johnson.

'I'd like to go into musical comedy,' said Peggy, who had black shingled hair, green eyes and the most lovely legs.

'You could too, Peggy,' I agreed, 'with your voice.'

Peggy was lucky, she came from a family who understood. Not like my parents who thought that Music Halls and Variety were not for good girls with a planned steady future. Peggy's family loved the kind of music I was wild about, not the classical music my father liked. Peggy's father played the mouth organ and they had a gramophone in a wooden cabinet in their front room. More than that, Peggy was having dancing lessons, she was actually being taught to tap dance.

'It's quite easy, Rose,' she explained to me as we practised in her front room with the carpet rolled back and the gramophone blaring, 'Yes sir, that's my baby'. 'Loosen up your ankle and then it's just two movements with your toe.'

Peggy wore the real thing, black sateen shoes, bow ties, with steel taps on the toes.

Winnie Johnson, who also lived in Petersfield Road, and had been at the Priory School with us joined our dance sessions. While Peggy was very pretty, Winnie was a beauty. At seventeen she had short curly, naturally blonde hair and big saucer blue eyes. No one had ever heard of sex-kittens in those days, but Winnie was the forerunner. She had that certain luminous quality that made her look as if she was lit up from inside. Wherever Winnie went the boys weren't far behind.

She too, was stage struck, but I'd say of the three of us Peggy was the one with the sure-fire talent. We were all very serious and single-minded; determined to get up on that stage behind the footlights. We didn't know how we were going to do it, but we were quite sure we'd get there.

'Couldn't we be chorus girls?' suggested Winnie.

'My mother would have a fit,' I declared. All my comings and goings were monitored. As my mother told me, she trusted me, but she wanted to know where I went.

'We could wear black satin shorts and white sleeveless tops,' said Peggy who was working it all out, 'and we could call ourselves the Peters Sisters, you know after Petersfield Road.'

'You mean we'd be a dance team, real performers?' Then I came back to reality. 'What about my Mum?'

'You could tell her that we're dancing for charity,' declared Peggy, who was the brains of the outfit. 'Tell her that we're going to dance for church bazaars, old people's homes, things like that.'

Peggy had never said a truer word. In the end that's exactly where we did dance. We worked out a great routine, copied from a Hollywood film about night club hoofers, we came on arms swinging, feet tapping. When we were really good we offered our services to the Vicar of St Mary's, off Acton High Street. Our first date was for a Girl Guides' Rally. We also did church bazaars, Mother's Union meetings, Girl's Friendly Society parties and old people's homes. We didn't earn a penny. It was art for art's sake, but we enjoyed ourselves and had lots of free teas.

Our next brush with show business came when the Mayor of Acton opened a new Gaumont British cinema called the Globe. This time we were not offering our talents free and for nothing, there was money in it. The first prize for the Talent Contest to be conducted at the Globe Cinema was one pound sterling.

Peggy would sing, I would play the piano and Winnie would stage manage us. We couldn't miss. But first we had to find the right song. 'Something soulful,' said Winnie, 'Something to make them cry.'

As we both thought that Peggy was the most talented girl in the world and that she sang like an angel, we chose the top of the pops in those

40

days, 'All of Me'. It had everything, sentiment, sadness, heart throb. Peggy could certainly put it over. She sang that she'd been forsaken by her lover, she begged him to take her back, that she was no good without him. 'You took the part that once was my heart,' sang Peggy, 'so why not take all of me.'

'It's full of passion,' said Winnie, who was as virginal as Peggy and me. 'It's your song, Peggy.' Rehearsals began in our front room, because I had to play the piano, and we were the only household with a piano.

Friday night was Talent Night, our names were down, we were dressed to kill in our long dresses. Mine was blue taffeta up to the knees in front and down to the heels at the back, a little cape across the shoulders and a row of pink roses down the front. Peggy was in red chiffon, she looked stunning. Quietly confident the three of us stood in the wings waiting for the other contestants to sing their songs and then we should go on and wipe the board. We were absolutely certain that we were going to win.

The first contestant, a girl, sang 'Ramona' which we thought was a mistake. The applause was half-hearted. The man who came next wasn't bad, not as good as Peggy, of course, but not bad. He got plenty of applause.

Our turn. We walked on. Bowed. I sat at the piano. Winnie in the wings clasped her hands

41

and shook them above her head like a boxer. I looked out at the sea of faces. So this was what it was all about, this was really the big time. Supremely confident I began to play and then Peggy sang.

Winnie in the wings hopped up and down mouthing, 'Put your heart into it, Peggy.' Peggy obliged. There was a sob in her voice. The applause was lovely. We bowed and left the stage. Winnie hugged us. 'We've won,' she whispered, 'we must have won.'

A smart alec from Kilburn came on at the end. A boy with patent leather hair and wide Oxford bags. He sang the song from the new talkie, *The Singing Fool*. He did everything that Al Jolson had done, but more so. He got down on his knees, he begged, he pleaded, he wiped the floor for his Sonny Boy. The applause was deafening.

'He's got friends in the audience,' said Winnie sourly.

'It's not fair,' I agreed. 'Bringing his friends. Nevermind, we'll win next time.'

We scoured the suburban cinemas for Talent Contests. You could only appear once at each cinema, but this was the heyday of the cinema and there were plenty of them. Peggy sang 'All of Me' at every contest. We never won. We always thought we should have done. The trouble, we decided, was that the winner always brought his friends with him, and the winner was always a man!

Peggy, I would say, had many talents, even if she didn't get her name in lights. I honestly think that Peggy failed in show business because she was a good girl and wouldn't sleep with the small time men at the bottom of the ladder, for that was the way it often was in those days. Peggy married three times and from one of her marriages she had a daughter called Daphne. Daphne was also very talented, went on the stage and did get her name up in lights. She went to Italy with the show she was in, fell in love and married a very wealthy Italian.

Peggy went out to have a holiday with Daphne. One evening she was taken to a very high class party at a very high class restaurant. There was soft music, an attentive signor sitting next to her who came on with the hand kissing and the 'bella bellas'. After a few vinos, Peggy was well away. Eventually she got to her feet. She ignored the anxious gestures of her daughter. 'I am going to sing for you,' she announced.

The pianist played a chord and gave her an encouraging smile. Light opera, perhaps, or a little English ballad?

Peggy clasped her hands to her breast just as Winnie had rehearsed her all those years ago. 'All of me,' she sang, 'Why not take all of me.' She really put her heart into it. She belted out her torch song just like a real trooper.

The applause was rapturous, better than anything we ever got at the talent contests, but when her daughter got her home, she gave her hell.

★   ★   ★

Sandwiched between the exploits of the Three Peters Sisters and the Talent Contests came my first love affair. I met him at a dance. As Winnie was always saying, 'The only way to get a fella's arms around you in public, without being had up, is to dance with him.' Winnie and I both fell in love for the first time at the Cricklewood Palais de Danse.

After the dull streets of Acton an evening at a Palais de Danse was like going into Fairyland. A jewelled palace with soft lights and sweet music. A place where coloured lights flashed, where a globe of tiny mirrors revolved, showering diamonds of light on the dancers. But above all the Palais was the gateway to romance, where if you were lucky, you might dance in the arms of the boy of your dreams.

For a shilling entrance fee on Saturday night you had an enchanted evening. The ritual began with the girls seated on chairs or at little tables and the boys standing around in uncertain groups. The atmosphere was as decorous as a vicar's tea party to begin with. No alcohol was served, only lemonade drunk through a straw and coffee. The demarcation lines were firmly drawn. There were the good girls and the girls the boys talked about. If you acted 'cheap' and got yourself talked about, your chances of settling down in respectable marriage with a dancing partner sank to zero. We remained virgins because we wanted to get married, because we loved our parents and because it made life so much easier.

I knew that I danced well and I was never a wallflower. In fact on this Saturday night as soon as the music began there was a boy standing in front of me saying, 'May I have the pleasure?' He bowed. He was very well mannered and he smelled of eau de cologne. He was only two or three inches taller than my five foot three, but he was slim and lithe. I couldn't pin-point it exactly but he was different to the other boys I danced with. He, too, was about eighteen, but he didn't say, 'Do you come here often?' as they did, he said, 'Do you like this song, it's by an American called Irving Berlin?' To this day whenever I hear 'Because', I remember David.

It was instant attraction on both sides. I thought his fair, curly hair romantic, his different, almost foreign look exciting, and he told me I was an English Rose. David and his friend, who had taken a shine to Winnie, danced with us all evening. They bought us lemonade and asked if they could see us home.

45

'Not this time,' I said prudently.

'We'll be here next Saturday,' they said. 'You will come?'

On our way home I said to Winnie, 'I didn't catch your boyfriend's name.'

'Izzy,' said Winnie. 'Hasn't he got lovely eyes.'

'Izzy,' I remarked, 'that's a funny name.'

David was my boyfriend for almost a year. We went to the pictures together, for walks on Sunday afternoons and to dance clubs on Sunday evenings. Ours was the intense pure love of two seventeen-year-olds.

One evening he came calling for me and my father opened the door. Next day my father said to me, 'He's a nice boy but I wouldn't take him too seriously. It won't go on for ever, you know.'

'Oh, that's not true.'

'Rose, he's Jewish, isn't he? What about his family?'

'I don't know them. They live in Maida Vale and he works with his father in a hairdressing business.'

'That's just it. Jewish families aren't like us. They'll want David to settle down with one of his own kind.'

'David wouldn't do that. He loves me.'

'That might be so,' said my father gently, 'but let me give you some advice. Find some other boyfriends.'

I didn't tell David what my father had said, but all the time I had this little fear implanted at the back of my mind. I couldn't believe that he'd give me up if his father told him to. All right David's family, the Glickbergs, were different to us, they lived in a posh mansion block of flats, they had their own business, but our hearts were the same, weren't they, and we loved each other?

One night when David brought me home I could see that he was nervous. 'I shan't come round again,' he said diffidently.

'Is it because of your family?' It couldn't be anything else, because young as I was, I knew the depth of his feelings for me.

He nodded miserably. 'Someone told my father.'

At that moment I wished with all my heart that I could find the kind of words that would convince him that my love for him shouldn't be cast aside so easily. I couldn't. I had been right that first time, there was something alien about David that I could never understand.

I didn't get over him easily. I pined. I used to ask Winnie to go with me to the Cricklewood Palais and I'd sit at the little table hoping that the orchestra would play 'Because I love you' and I'd see David coming across the dance floor towards me. It didn't happen. I never saw David again.

I wasn't the only miserable one in our house.

47

My father had lost his job. It was the beginning of the Depression and the Gas Company started laying off the fitters.

Things weren't quite as bad as they'd been when he was out of a job after the 1918 war. Grace and I were at work. But he was the man of the house, he had to keep the home going. Although he was out of work for three solid years, he brought money to my mother every week. Any odd job going, my father would do it. He dug gardens, he worked as a caddy at the golf course at Southall. He mended furniture. My father's hands had always had special powers, they could take on jobs that others thought hopeless, and his clever fingers would join the parts together.

Now that he was out of work, he thought of a use to which he could put his hands that would combine with his love of sport. He'd always been a keen supporter of the Finchley Harriers, cross-country runners, and he often went up to their club in Cricklewood.

I came home from work one evening and he was busy in the scullery filling little bottles with oil. A saucepan was on the stove and the air was heavy with the smell of wintergreen.

'I'm making my own rubbing oils,' he told me. 'I'm learning about massage.'

'Who are you going to massage Dad,' I laughed, 'the Finchley Harriers?'

'That's right, my girl,' he said with

satisfaction. 'Go and look at the books on the table. I've been down to the public library.'

There was a big book on anatomy. He watched me as I turned the pages and looked at the illustrations. 'I've got to learn all about the direction and action of the muscles,' he told me, his thin face alive with enthusiasm, 'and when I understand that I shall read the book on massage.'

He did exactly what he said. He became a first-rate masseur and trainer to the Finchley Harriers.

*   *   *

Perhaps it was something to do with the unsettled way I felt after the end of my relationship with David, but I decided that invisible mending at Eastman's was giving me headaches and I looked for another job.

I found one at a nearby factory. I was to earn a pound a week, making teddy bears. I started work not knowing what I was to do, but quite sure I should love working among these soft cuddly toys. After I had stuffed my first teddy bear I changed my opinion.

I was given an instrument with a long wooden handle and a steel rod. Getting the knack of winding straw into a tight ball round this tool was quite a performance and then the teddy bear stuffing proper would begin, forcing straw into the body and arms and legs, and finally pushing sawdust into the nooks and crannies. As I worked the row of teddy bear heads stared blankly at me. Now that I knew their secrets, teddy bears no longer had any fascination for me. Once you've stuffed a teddy bear you never feel the same way about them again.

I knew I'd made a terrible mistake but what with my father out of work I felt I could not leave this job and look for another. However, meeting Henry showed me a way out.

Henry was an older man. I met him when I went to the optician's to see if I needed glasses because of the headaches I developed over the invisible mending. I hardly noticed him when I went into the shop, this dapper confident man with well-brilliantined hair and horn-rimmed spectacles. Anyone over 25 was an older man to 18-year-old me, and when Henry turned out to be 30, I thought he was practically in his dotage.

As it happened there was nothing wrong with my eyes, but by the time I left the shop Henry had been introduced and was showing what I took to be a fatherly interest in me.

'Can I give you a lift home?' he asked.

A lift? I stared at him. Did this mean that he had a motor car? No one I knew had ever owned a car. Even the doctor did his rounds on a bicycle. Henry turned out to be the owner of a bull-nosed Morris two-seater. I was quite overwhelmed, but I had enough sense to ask him to drop me off at the corner of Petersfield Road, otherwise too many lace curtains would twitch and too many tongues would wag.

'I'm not sure I like it,' said my father, after he'd met Henry for the first time. 'Bit too old for you Rose, and he'll be set in his ways. There's something funny about a man who hasn't found a wife by the time he's 30.'

Going out with Henry showed me a slice of life I had never seen before. We ate dinner at Maxim's, a Chinese restaurant off Leicester Square where you not only ate bean sprouts and spring rolls but also danced to an orchestra. We had tea by the river at Richmond and supper at the Ace of Spades Night Club on the Kingston By-pass where Henry took his own bottle of gin, but I stuck firmly to orange juice.

That evening I told him about my problem with the teddy bears.

'Rose,' said Henry, pouring himself another large gin. 'How would you like to become an optician's assistant?'

I wasn't sure. I liked the new affluent life that Henry showed me but Henry always came with the package. I liked him, I even allowed a chaste kiss now and then, but the thought of anything more seemed vaguely incestuous, like embracing an uncle. Sometimes I thought longingly of the small, golden-haired David and the sheer happiness of whirling under the coloured lights at the Cricklewood Palais.

'I'd teach you the profession,' urged Henry. 'At first you could just carry my case of sample spectacles and learn how to use the test card. I'll pay you one pound a week, so you won't be out of pocket.'

It was a tempting offer. I'd reached the pitch where I was becoming sadistic with the little brown bears, jabbing them cruelly, stuffing their chests with sawdust until they squeaked and deliberately moving their eyes so that they would leer frighteningly at the kiddiwinks. But I knew quite well that my mother and father wouldn't be pleased. Like me they'd think there was something vaguely suspicious about the deal.

'Don't tell them just yet,' Henry suggested. 'Give yourself a chance to get used to the new arrangement.'

After a week as optician's mate, I wasn't at all sure that it was such a good idea. It meant that Henry and I spent eight hours of every day together and he was becoming rather possessive. He now talked of 'settling down'. One Sunday he took me to visit his sister in Ealing. A nice motherly woman who seemed more like an aunt than a prospective sister-in-law. I felt that I had strayed into the wrong scene, peopled with kindly souls who were trying to draw me into their geriatric way of life.

At the end of my second week I knew little more about ophthalmology, but I had visited most of the opticians' shops in north and west London. Henry saw that I was becoming restive and told me he would teach me to drive. After a short driving lesson Henry parked the car in a quiet corner. It was getting late. My mother always expected me home from the teddy bear factory at half past five, and here we were miles away near Hanger Lane in Ealing.

'What about getting engaged?' said Henry unexpectedly.

'Engaged?' I repeated. I knew with absolute certainty that I did not want to get married to Henry. I'd had enough of being an optician's mate too. I'd rather go home first.

Henry's hand rested on my knee. His mouth nuzzled my right ear.

I drew back and gave his hand a shove.

'If we're going to get married,' said Henry complacently, 'You'll have to learn to be a little more affectionate.' He renewed his insidious attack, an arm around my waist, his mouth near my right eyebrow and the most shocking thing of all, his hand under my skirt up my thigh.

I gave a shrill cry of outrage and began to wrestle. Henry took this as encouragement. What shocking thing was his left hand doing? My cries grew louder, I jabbed, I kicked, and in the end I found I had opened the car door and fallen out. I picked myself up and ran as fast as I could away from Henry.

It was a long way from Hanger Lane to Acton. I had to walk as I had no money. Henry hadn't paid me my week's wages. When I eventually arrived home Henry's car was there parked outside my home. He sat with my father and mother in the front room.

'Rose,' he cried jumping to his feet. 'You had me terribly worried.'

'Wherever have you been, Rose?' demanded my father. 'Is something wrong?'

I pointed an accusing finger at Henry, 'Ask him!' I cried dramatically. 'That man put his hand up my skirt. That's what he did.'

'Out!' My father flung the front door open wide. 'Out! And don't ever come back.'

'The filthy beast,' said my mother, as Henry exited.

At the back of my mind I knew I was laying it on a bit thick. Poor old Henry was really a very nice man, kind and generous, with very honourable intentions. After all he'd asked me to marry him before he'd laid a finger on me. However, I had no time for remorse, I was so overwhelmed with this feeling of relief and happiness. I was free again. I could go back and join the boys and girls.

CHAPTER FOUR

THOSE GOLDEN SUMMERS WHEN I WAS YOUNG

My new husband sat bolt upright in bed. He fumbled under the bedclothes. 'Oh, my god,' he gasped, 'it's lost.' He turned to me, anxiety etched on his handsome face. 'Rose, get up! I've got to take you to hospital!'

Hospital on our wedding night! My eyes filled with tears. Was this why I'd kept myself pure and virginal, to end up on the operating table? On the first night of my honeymoon, too. My past life suddenly swam before my eyes. I should never have pinched him from Ivy. Maybe I should never have left the teddy bear factory and Henry.

But that had been over a year ago. I'd been an embryo film actress and chewing gum distributor since then. Tucking sample packets of American chewing gum through suburban letter boxes hadn't been much of a job, especially when it rained. My downfall and instant dismissal from the chewing gum route was caused by the unkind elements. I shuffled along, head bent in the drizzling rain, large drops from the privet hedges going down the back of my collar when I bumped into a fat friendly woman.

'Wot you delivering, love?' she asked.

'Chewing Gum.'

'I've got eight kids. They like chewing gum.'

I pressed eight samples into her hand.

'Here, tell you wot I'll do. Hand me over your supply for this road and I'll get my kids to deliver it.'

I should have known better, but I had nearly finished my satchelful and the thought of the warm fire at home and the big black kettle on the hob waiting to brew the tea, beckoned me. I emptied the sack into her shopping basket. My act of philanthropy was spotted by an observant supervisor and I got the sack.

My next job was in ice cream. 'Stop me and buy one.' Walls Ice Cream men trundling along on their tricycles were a welcome sight in the thirties. They were a friendly crowd at the ice cream depot in North Acton and it didn't take long before I could stack the ice cream containers that fitted on the bikes with the best of them. The management were easy going, and when trade was slack no one minded if you took the odd day off.

'Rose,' said Peggy, my girlfriend with all the talent, the one I used to accompany at the Talent Contests, 'how about going into films?'

'Well I can take tomorrow off if that's any good?'

'Spiffing! They want extras down at the

Shepherd's Bush studios, and if we get up at the crack of dawn we can be at the top of the queue.'

We got up at five-thirty next day, but unfortunately there was already a queue of people who had got up even earlier outside the studios. As soon as the window went up at eight at the studio gates the queue moved rapidly inside. Fifty extras were engaged for crowd work, twenty dress extras for a ballroom scene, and then the man started to draw down the window. He stopped. 'Oh, we want four waitresses.'

Peggy and I now at the top of the queue were in. We spent the day serving tea, coffee and sandwiches to the crew and extras. We didn't see much of the action, but we were each paid a pound, and we were part of the film world. Even more important, we now had our contacts and the news that extras were needed was passed on by word of mouth.

Being a film extra in those days, without a union to watch out for your rights, was rugged. The hours you worked were elastic, if the director wanted to work until midnight, you sat around until he was satisfied. We were young enough to find it fun, and then there was always the impossible chance that one day the camera would pan back to the crowd scene, settle on your photogenic little face and you'd be offered a bit part.

There were no agencies to find people work in bit parts or as extras in those days. And Peggy and I were absolutely sure that the only way you got on in the film world was to say 'yes'. It wasn't the big names who wanted you to sleep with them, it was the little names, the hangers on around the important people. Peggy and I were often propositioned.

'See those two blokes over there,' Peggy would say, 'Well the little one in the check cap says he's Michael Balcon's cousin, and he can get us work as dancers in a new Gainsborough production.'

'Michael Balcon's cousin, my Aunt Fanny. I know that man, he used to have a barrow down at the Bush. What's he want anyway?'

'Three guesses?' sighed Peggy. 'But I already said, no.'

I don't say we were right. Even if we'd fornicated ourselves silly, maybe we wouldn't have risen above the rank of extra, but our firm conviction remained. There wasn't a virgin left in the film business—apart from us, of course.

As well as the silver screen, my ambitions were turned towards ballroom dancing. Winnie, my other friend and I, now had our regular partners for Saturday nights and Sunday club nights at the ballrooms that were within easy distance of Acton. There was the Carlton, Shepherd's Bush, Acton Town Hall, the Hammersmith Palais, and my favourite, Kew

Palais. Although we were on nodding terms with most of the young people who frequented the dance halls, we stayed in our own fierce little groups, intent on winning the prizes for best dancers; things like a bottle of port, a Dundee cake, or a box of biscuits.

I thought that Kew Palais de Danse on the other side of Kew Bridge was one of the prettiest dance halls. It was at Kew that a boy kicked my ankle and because he did not apologise as requested was reprimanded by the boys in my group. There was never any scuffling or fighting in the Palais. Any sign of bad behaviour and the stewards would move in, but once outside that was another matter. Although, even then, the quarrels were mostly verbal.

Winnie's boyfriend, (nicknamed Waggie, because his name was Charles, and everyone called Charles was known as Wag) had a phenomenal hand. Although it was perfectly normal in every way, it never seemed to feel pain, perhaps it was devoid of nerves, because no matter how hard he used it, he suffered not a twinge. So Waggie's reputation as having a fist that packed a real wallop was well known.

After the dance the boy who'd kicked my ankle was cornered and told to apologise. When he saw Waggie and his fist, he did so quickly. As the altercation was going on, a tall elegant couple passed by. I recognised them. I'd always admired the way they looked and the professionalism of their dancing, and I wished for a moment that they hadn't seen me.

The following Saturday in the Paul Jones when the music stopped and I found myself opposite the tall young man. As we danced he said, 'Aren't you the girl who was the cause of the trouble on the bridge last week?'

'Goodness, no,' I lied shamelessly, 'that was Winnie.'

He was a very tall young man, about six foot one and I had to crick my neck to look up at him. He looked down at me and smiled. He had dimples. With his sleek, well-brushed brown hair and thin moustache, I thought he was incredibly handsome.

Later on in the cloakroom while Winnie and I carefully applied our Tangee lipstick and shared a dab from another girl's bottle of Californian Poppy, I saw the tall young man's partner come in, halt in front of the mirror and dab her thin aristocratic nose with a swansdown puff. I tried not to stare, but to me she was as sophisticated as a page out of *Vogue* magazine. Her black hair was drawn back from a centre parting to a bun, she had dangling earrings and a Spanish-type red dress. The Latin look was in that year.

'Do you know who she is?' I whispered to Winnie.

Winnie smoothed down her eyebrows and

gave her a quick glance. 'Her name's Ivy, and she works in the Guinea shop.' Guinea shops, where every dress or coat cost not more than twenty-one shillings, were springing up everywhere.

I was ten minutes late getting home that night. My father solemnly locked up at eleven o'clock. My mother would put her head round our bedroom door and call 'Goodnight girls' to her sleeping daughters. Sister Grace was always in on time and if I was still out, she arranged a life-like dummy with a pillow and bolster in the double bed next to her. She also left the window that faced directly onto the road up about an inch, I'd take off my shoes, lift up the window very slowly—these old sashcord windows could creak—and climb through. I was never caught.

Tonight I climbed through, undressed and slipped into bed beside Grace. 'I met a very nice boy tonight,' I said in an undertone.

'What's his name?'

'I don't know.'

'Does he like you?'

'He might. Trouble is he's got a girlfriend.'

Grace yawned, 'That shouldn't stop you, Rose.'

The tall young man's name was Burt Neighbour. He was twenty years old and lived in Kilburn. He must have liked me because the next time we met at Kew Palais, he came over and asked me for a dance. He was just as nice as

I remembered. There was nothing conceited about him and yet I thought he was the handsomest man in the ballroom. He laughed a lot, and when his eyes narrowed and the dimples showed each side of his mouth my knees felt weak.

Of course the trouble was Ivy. He'd been going out with her for some months. And Ivy was not only gorgeous to look at, she was a sweet girl. When I met her I liked her straight off. She and Burt were soon part of our group and we met every Saturday night, going from one Palais de Danse to another.

Usually there were no alcoholic drinks available, but at the Kew Palais there was a bar. Ivy liked a gin and 'it'. As Burt and I swayed to the strains of 'You were meant for me', out of the corner of my eye I saw Ivy and her partner disappearing into the bar for her favourite gin and Italian vermouth.

'I don't drink,' I said to Burt, à propos of what was in my mind.

'Neither do I,' said Burt.

'I don't feel the need, do you?'

'No,' said Burt, and his hand pressed mine just a little more firmly.

'I think it clouds the brain.' I'd read that, and I knew it sounded good.

We danced on, united in our mutual sobriety. I was making progress. We won the quickstep contest that night and were handed a cut-glass vase. 'Perhaps Ivy should have it,' I said innocently, 'for her bottom drawer?' Burt gave me a hunted look.

The three of us, Burt, Ivy and I, knew perfectly well what was happening, but Burt had to make the first move. When, one night, Burt asked me if I'd like to go to the pictures with him, that was the breakthrough. But I did have Ivy on my conscience.

'What about Ivy?' I had to ask.

'There's nothing between us,' said Burt with male logic. 'We're not engaged or anything.'

It was Ivy herself who settled matters. It happened in the cloakroom, the only place where we were completely ourselves, no longer acting our parts in front of the boys. We stood in front of the mirror together, and I pressed my fingers into the curves of my Marcel wave and Ivy fidgeted with a little black kiss curl.

'You like Burt, don't you?' she said. Our eyes met in the mirror.

I gave her a half smile, too unsure to say anything.

'And he likes you.'

My smile became rather strained. Was she going to ask me to keep away from him? 'I hope he does,' I said at last.

Ivy sighed, her beautiful face looked pensive. 'Well, if that's the way it is, then I think you'd better have him, don't you?'

Burt who had no idea that he'd been formally

handed over in the ladies' cloakroom took me to the pictures. I knew that Ivy was upset and that I was the reason, but when you're nineteen and in love, you're in too much of a hurry to stop and nurse the wounded. Ivy got over Burt quite soon. She found another boyfriend, and the six of us, Winnie, Wag, and Burt and I, and Ivy and her new beau, used to go around together.

In the summer we all went on the river. The waters of the Thames in those days were truly lovely. Our punts would glide gracefully through the tranquil waters; there were no powerful motor vessels as there are now, to swamp the small boats with their wash.

On Saturday afternoon, if the weather was good, we'd meet at the bus stop, the boys in white flannels and white pullovers and the girls in frilly voile dresses and large shady hats, and off we'd go with our rugs and cushions and portable gramophone down to Teddington Lock. We all dressed as carefully as if we were going to a garden party.

At Teddington Lock the boys would hire two punts, at about a pound each, two couples in each punt, usually Winnie and Wag shared our punt, with Ivy, her beau and another couple in the other. The gramophone was wound up and to the strains of music Waggie would punt us down to Laleham. Burt had a lovely singing voice—to me he sounded just as good as Bing Crosby. We'd tie up at the river bank and have the first picnic, the food that our mothers had cooked.

But the most exciting part of the expedition came at night when the canvas covers would be drawn over the punts, four girls would settle down in one punt for the night and the four boys in the other. Giggling and whispering, terribly excited at roughing it on the river it would be a long time before we fell asleep, and even then we'd be awakened by the boys poking reeds through the holes in the canvas to frighten us into thinking that they were rats. But that was as far as it went. We fell into innocent untroubled dreams, and I think it was better that way.

I had the happiest youth imaginable. I wouldn't have changed it. I had little money (two shillings and sixpence pocket money didn't go far), very few possessions, but I had every conceivable joy of the spirit. I had romance, nothing for me could have been more romantic than dancing in Burt Neighbour's arms wearing a new long dress my mother had made for me.

I'd started my bottom drawer, the bits and pieces a girl collected before she married; a pair of embroidered pillowcases, a lace tea cloth, and dressing table set. Burt had asked me to marry him and now I dreamt of three piece suites and the home we would make together. Perhaps I was misguided, gullible, influenced by the stories I read in the women's magazines, but I was happy in my innocence and in some ways the quality of my life was better then than it has ever been. Perhaps I enjoyed those golden summers so much just because I was young, but they are sweet memories.

Who knew what the future was going to bring the four girls who giggled in the punt those far off summer nights? It was as well we didn't know. A year later Winnie, luscious and blonde, fell in love with a man from a completely different background, he was upper-class from a wealthy family. His mother did everything to stop him marrying a poor girl from Petersfield Road, but she couldn't break up the romance. When she died, however, she managed it. Her son inherited her vast fortune and soon after he left Winnie and went back to his former way of life. The last time I saw Winnie she was working as a barmaid in Fleet Street.

Ivy, Burt's one time girlfriend, although she had plenty of boyfriends never married, and Connie the fourth girl in the punt, who I always thought looked like a film star, had a breakdown and was taken to a mental institution from where she never emerged again. She may still be there.

Burt's mother, a large domineering lady let me know her opinion of our approaching marriage in one short sentence. 'Burt's too young!' I don't think she had very much against me, but in common with a lot of mothers she just didn't want her son to get married. Burt's father, on the other hand, welcomed me. He enjoyed giving me a smacking kiss and calling me his little Rosy Posy. Mr Neighbour was a master tailor with his own shop in Beak Street, off Regent Street. I thought they should have been quite well off, but they weren't.

'It's the horses,' said Burt's mother gloomily, in one of her rare confidential chats. 'All his money goes on the horses.'

I suppose I should have pricked up my ears, but no matter if she'd told me that Burt came from a long line of confirmed gamblers and that Burt might one day put all our money on the horses, I wouldn't have worried. To my mind the love of a good woman could overcome any obstacle. We were deeply in love and as soon as Burt had saved enough we were going to be married. I was moving up in the world. I wasn't expected to provide any material possessions. In the thirties, in our society, a man paid for everything; it was the man's duty to look after the little woman. Only in the direst circumstances would a wife be expected to go out to work, as my mother had done.

Burt was a salesman at Keith Prowse, the well known establishment that sold theatre tickets, sheet music and gramophone records. Burt's job was glamorous and to me part of show business. In a roundabout way it was because of Keith Prowse that we were able to get married when Burt was twenty-one. He bought one of the firm's raffle tickets and won first prize—a dear little Morris sports car.

'D'you know what we'll do with this car, Rose?' he said to me as soon as we heard of his good fortune.

I knew he couldn't drive and motor cars cost money to keep.

'We're going to sell it and save the money. We'll have enough to furnish a home.'

'More than enough,' I exclaimed. With the two hundred pounds we should get we'd be rich.

'What d'you say to us opening our business? If I keep on saving we could have a shop where we'd sell sheet music and gramophone records!'

We were both crazy about dance music, it would be like realising a dream. At that moment it seemed that the world was ours for the taking. And we were absolutely sure of the happy ending.

*　　*　　*

A few days before I got married my mother took me aside for a little talk. My sister and I had been brought up in the prudish atmosphere of most respectable families. Although our home was full of love and affection, there had never been any talk of sex. Even poor Aunt

68

Agnes's misdemeanours had been kept secret from us. Nice girls didn't even talk among their friends about such things. We giggled and nudged each other in the ribs, but we only had the vaguest idea what a smutty joke was about. I didn't know how babies were conceived or born, I didn't even know what a man looked like without his clothes on.

Sometimes my mother had taken care of a little boy called Reuben while his mother spent periods of time in hospital. When he was bathed in the tin tub in front of the fire on a Saturday night, before she lifted him out of the tub to dry him, my mother would say 'Now girls, turn your backs.'

I know that my mother was acutely embarrassed about what she had to tell me, but she had decided that it was her duty to prepare her daughter for holy wedlock.

'Rose,' she began rather shakily. 'Did you ever wonder why you didn't have a brother?'

I couldn't say that I did, but I hoped she wasn't going to spring a long lost one on me now.

'Your father and I only had two children because that was all we could afford.'

'I didn't mind Mum.' At last I was beginning to see which way the conversation was leading.

'You don't want to start having babies as soon as you're married, do you, Rose?'

Indeed I didn't. The last thing I wanted was a

baby to clutter up the sparkling future Burt and I were planning.

'Well, all you have to do to stop having babies is to go along to Mr Smart, the chemist, tell him that you're getting married and ask for a box of Rendal's pills.'

I was overcome with dismay. I hardly knew Mr Smart.

'Oh, I couldn't do that Mum.'

'You do as I say Rose. He'll know what you want.'

I thought that if Grace came along to hold my hand I might manage to get the words out, but what then? 'How many of these pills do I have to take Mum?'

My mother moistened her lips, but then her courage failed her. 'You can ask Burt about that when the time comes. He'll know.' She smiled at me. 'I want you to have a happy life. It's not fair on a girl to start a baby straight away.' She made a final attempt to tell me more about the facts of life. 'Is there anything else you want to know?'

There was, but I was too shy to ask my mother and I knew she'd be too shy to tell me. I'd never seen a man undressed and I was full of curiosity. I'd just have to leave it until my wedding night. Which I could see was going to be a night packed with revelations.

It was good news all the way in August 1932, the month when I got married. My father had a permanent job at Napier's, a nearby factory. They made aero engines and all the order books were full. Because of this my father said there was certainly going to be a war. How he got this inside information seven years before war was declared I don't know. But as always, he was right. For four years he'd done odd jobs to keep our heads above water and now he had a permanent job and was happy.

Just five minutes' walk away from my home we had found a flat in Berrymead Gardens. It was very much the same kind of place where I'd lived all my life, a bottom flat with no bath and an outside toilet, but we thought it was palatial. We had a lovely Turkish pattern carpet down in the front room, a radiogram and a brand new three piece leather suite. In the bedroom we had matched oak furniture that was meant to last and for the first time in my life I had a real dressing table with a cut-glass vanity set.

The week before the wedding my mother and Aunt Rose prepared the wedding breakfast. The trifles and the jellies stood in a row on the flagstones of the scullery to keep cool and the wedding cake was in a big cardboard box. Then the lady in the flat upstairs said that as her front room was larger than ours, why didn't we borrow it?

When I look at the wedding photographs that were taken in the playground of the Priory School over the way it all comes back. The bridesmaids, Grace and Burt's sister, Winifred, in their pale blue georgette dresses, the white lace dress I wore with orange blossoms pinned to the veil. And as the photographer moved the shutter of his camera I remember thinking that this was the happiest day of my life.

Nothing marred the happy day. Not even when we came out of St Mary's church after the ceremony and saw my new mother-in-law arriving. It did cross my mind that she'd left it a bit late. She blamed the traffic, but as my mother said afterwards, 'What a story! We sent her a Daimler a good half hour before we left, and even if she'd pushed the car all the way herself she could have made it on time.'

We all sat down in the front room upstairs at a long trestle table covered with white damask cloths and ate the delicious meal my mother and Aunt Rose had prepared. Legs of lamb with mint sauce, roast potatoes and runner beans. Afterwards when we cut the wedding cake it was open house to all our friends and the drink flowed.

What with the cost of the wedding, furnishing the house and saving for the shop, we didn't go away on a honeymoon. And at last there was I on my wedding night wearing my new peach satin nightdress, sitting up in bed watching Burt undress.

'What are you staring at?' Burt asked. 'Haven't you seen a man undress before?'

'No!' I replied honestly.

He removed his shirt and trousers and stood there unveiled. I couldn't help laughing. He looked at me with a pained expression. 'What's so funny?' he asked.

I tried to stop laughing, 'It's just that I thought you'd be the same colour all over, but you're not.'

Burt in his new striped pyjamas moved to the bed. From under the pillow I produced my box of 'Rendal's.'

'Put those away, we shan't need them.' Burt spoke as an experienced man of the world. 'I've got something of my own.' It turned out afterwards that he wasn't as experienced as he made out and he didn't make a very good job of putting it on.

I'm sure that Burt knew little more about birth control than I did. We were both virgins, but our first attempt at love making went rather well. We were very much in love and afterwards we lay in each other's arms knowing that at last we were really husband and wife.

Suddenly Burt shot upright. He searched frantically under the bedclothes. 'Oh my God,' he turned to me. 'Rose, get up! I've got to take you to hospital.'

'Why?' I gasped.

'Because I've lost it and God only knows where it's gone.'

'Lost what?'

'Something I wore to stop babies.'

'I haven't got it. I'm sure I haven't got it.'

We flung back the bedclothes and started to search. Eventually there it was under the bed.

Our laughter went on and on. At last Burt said. 'D'you know what they say. Wearing a french letter is just like eating a chocolate with the wrapping paper on. Come on, Rose, where did you put those pills?'

CHAPTER FIVE

I SOLD ROMANCE AT SIXPENCE A TIME

It was Carnival time on Epsom Downs. The Pearly King and Queen, their costumes dazzling in the sun, led a procession on donkeys through the cheering crowd. The music from the fair on the hill, the steam organ booming out 'Blaze Away', the yells from the sideshows, and shouts of the Bookies made up a crescendo of noises this Derby Day. The Gypsy women, in emerald and scarlet skirts, swung their baskets of white heather towards us, and their caravans . . . I'd never seen such caravans, made of traditional wood and painted red with yellow wheels.

Prince Monolulu, the aristocrat of tipsters in

his feather head-dress and Ethiopian Jodpurs, picked me out in the crowd. 'I gotta horse,' he shouted and 'I'll give it to this pretty girl for nothing.' He bent his grey-brown wrinkled face near to mine and whispered in my ear. What he said I couldn't hear for the burst of laughter around us. I clung closer to Burt's arm.

We had come down by train from Victoria to Tattenham Corner this lovely day in May for the 1933 Derby. Because it was my outing Burt came with me onto the Downs rather than go into one of the stands where the horse-racers congregated. We had a picnic lunch in our carrier bag and a day in the country ahead of us. On the hill behind the refreshment tent the crowd was thinner. We stretched out on the green, sweet-smelling grass and Burt thumbed through his race card.

'I've got a feeling,' he said. 'It's going to be my lucky day.'

I rolled over onto my stomach and looked at him fondly. We had been married for just ten months and no girl in the world had a better husband. Burt was kind, generous and so easy to live with. He was full of happiness that was infectious.

Down below, near the rails the bookmakers were calling their odds. Their voices floated up the hill. 'Two to one, bar one.' 'Five to four the field.'

Burt got to his feet. 'I'll go down and look at

the prices, then I'll come back and take you to see the first race. There's the winning post down there. Look, can you see it?'

We were down there by the winning post for the big race of the afternoon, the Derby. Burt was hanging over the rails yelling 'Come on Hyperion!' And the roars of the crowd as Hyperion won were ear-splitting. Laughing, almost beside himself with excitement, Burt threw his arms around me, 'We've won! We've won, Rose.'

I went back and sat on the grass by the refreshment tent while Burt collected his winnings. I watched him coming back, wending his way through the people lying on the grass. His handsome face was radiant. It did my heart good to see how much he loved horse racing. He stretched out beside me. 'Close your eyes and give me your hand,' he ordered. I obeyed. Paper that was stiff and crackled was placed on my palm. When I opened my eyes I saw there were two of them. Two large white five pound notes, each one neatly folded into four. I picked them up carefully and raised my eyes to his.

'It's yours, Rose! So that you'll remember this Derby Day.'

Ten pounds! I couldn't believe it. In 1933, ten pounds was a deposit on a house. It bought a fur coat, a real one. It took you away on a week's holiday. It was riches and Burt had won it on a horse.

76

Burt laughed at the expression on my face. 'See what a clever husband, you've got. Surprised, eh?'

I was surprised, but I was also frightened. It seemed too easy. That horse Hyperion had brought us this money, but what if he hadn't won? I'd seen the odds. Hyperion was six to one. How much had Burt put on to win all this money. Two pounds, maybe, and two pounds was a week's wages.

'Put it away somewhere safe,' Burt ordered. 'I told you it was my lucky day. I'm going straight through the card.' I could see he was in a fever to go, to be back down there by the rails with the punters, the bookmakers and the noise of the crowd. 'Back in ten minutes,' he said as he got up to leave again. 'You all right?'

I was all right and I had enough sense to hold my tongue, but I longed to ask him to stay with me, to do what he'd said we'd do, have a day out in the country. I wanted to see all those sights again that we'd passed as we came from Tattenham Corner, the Gypsy caravans, the side-shows, the jellied eel stands. I wanted to forget the nagging question in my head. How much money was Burt putting on the horses? What if he should lose? It was much more than we could afford, I knew that. I could hear my mother-in-law's voice when she spoke about her husband, 'He puts all our money on the horses . . .'

I suppose there is a turning point in everyone's life. But that was the first time I saw the gambling fever in Burt's eyes, and the first time I felt the fear, that never again completely left me, that when Burt gambled he lost all sense of proportion. Money . . . the pounds, the shillings and the pence we watched so carefully in our everyday life; the pence we counted out for bus fares, the shillings for rent and the pounds that were so few, became like fairy gold to be squandered. He didn't want to win the money, Burt was a generous man, he wanted those five minutes of ecstacy when his horse was in front winning.

★   ★   ★

I used to tell Burt that he fancied himself as a crooner. He played the piano at Keith Prowse for the customers, as happy as a sandboy, singing all the latest hits so that they'd buy the sheet music or the gramophone record. He was always singing at home.

'You and Bing Crosby,' I'd say, 'for you two it's always "June in January".'

They nicknamed him Felix at Keith Prowse because of the way he walked up and down his hands behind his back just like Felix, the black cat, in the popular cartoon. It helped him to think, he said, helped him to plan for the future. He'd worked at Keith Prowse since he was fifteen and he loved his job. All day long he worked with songs and dance music, advising the musicians who came in about what was new because Burt had an instinct for a tune that was going to sell well. There was no top of the pops then, but Burt could pick out a hit well before anyone else.

Burt should have been in the popular music explosion in the swinging sixties when a working-class boy could have catapulted to the top. He had all the ideas for promoting music that surged forward thirty years later. But when he was young the only way Burt knew to make money in the music world was to open a shop selling gramophone records and sheet music.

A few months after we were married a friend of his who had a shop in Shepherd's Bush told him about a new covered market that was opening in Slough. One Sunday in November we took the Green Line bus and went over to see it. In those days Slough was a little country town twenty miles west of London. The farming community around came into Slough to shop, industry was opening up around the town, there was even a small trading estate and the prospects for the future were good. Nowadays, Slough has a population of over 100,000 and the giant Jumbo Jets from Heathrow Airport thunder overhead, but then it was a small town with big opportunities for a young couple from Acton who were going to fill the market with music.

The market hall in the High Street looked very smart and new. There were two rows of lock-up shops and it was covered by a glass roof. Quite a few of the shops had already been taken but there were two good positions left on either side near the top. We stood gazing at them trying to make up our mind which one was better.

'What are you going to sell?' asked a voice behind us. A man and a small fair-haired woman looked at us expectantly.

'Music,' we spoke together.

The man who was tall and broad, visibly relaxed. 'That's all right then. We're in the linen business. What say you take this one and we have that one over there?'

It was the first time we met Ted Gould and Rita his wife. While the two men walked over to inspect the other shop, Rita and I chatted together. 'We should do well here,' she told me. 'What with the Christmas trade coming up.' We smiled at each other. I liked her straight away. I felt instinctively that she was a good, kind woman and that we should be friends.

Ted and Rita already owned two other shops. They were leaving a manager in their Edgware shop while they built up the trade here in Slough. I always remember the first cold day in December when we opened. There was no heating and we all wore our hats and coats and gloves.

'Don't forget,' cautioned Rita, 'always stand in front of your shop to catch the custom, but make sure you keep your cash box hidden at the back of the shop.' Rita showed me all the ropes. She was a quiet, naturally reserved woman, but when she had a customer she seemed to develop another personality. To see Rita selling linen sheets and pillowcases, holding out an embroidered tablecloth to a farmer's wife was a revelation. 'You see this embroidery,' she'd say, 'it's all done by the nuns in Madeira. They sit in their convents working by lamplight until the fine needlework makes them go blind.'

'Is that true, Rita?' I'd ask her, 'do they really go blind?'

'I hope not,' she said. 'Those tablecloths came from a back alley off the Commercial Road, but I like to send the customers home with a little story. They take more care of it if they think some poor old nun's done it. And at the price I sell it's a give-away.'

In our shop there was no big sales talk. Burt advised the customers and played the songs they wanted on the gramophone. I wrapped up the sheet music, sold the boxes of gramophone needles, took in the radios that needed their batteries re-charging. The stock moved out rapidly and Burt kept re-ordering for the Christmas rush. Burt had given up his job at Keith Prowse and fitting out and stocking the lock-up shop had taken most of our capital. It was important that we had a quick turnover, and very important that we paid our bills promptly so that we could keep ordering new stock.

I remember one of the big sellers that Christmas was a Noel Coward song 'Mad about the Boy'. I sang it just as everyone did that year but when I thought about the lyric I sometimes wondered why it was so popular. It was about a middle-aged woman who had fallen madly in love with a handsome young film star. The only time she ever saw him was on the silver screen, but the sight of him melted her heart and he filled her life with both unhappiness and joy. I think it was the sad haunting tune which made it such a hit.

There we were right in the middle of the Depression with records and sheet music pouring out the misery of it all. And yet they sold like hot cakes. 'Buddie Can you Spare a Dime' sold and sold on both sides of the Atlantic. Putting it to music does make people forget their troubles; our success in that first month proved that.

Other people might be unemployed but Burt and I worked as we'd never done before. Up at six to catch the bus to Slough, opening up the shop filling the display stand with fresh sheet music, running the radios round to the dealer in the side street who re-charged them for us, arranging the piles of gramophone records in their thin brown paper slip covers, then popping the kettle on in the cubbyhole behind the shop to make a quick cup of tea before the first customer arrived. By ten in the morning the arcade was full of jostling crowds of shoppers. It went on like that every day until Christmas Eve. At night we'd get on the bus taking us home, our new cash box heavy with coppers and shillings on my lap and before we reached the first village, I'd be asleep, my head on Burt's shoulder.

In the New Year trade slackened off slightly and we had time to look around. Burt took a trip up to Keith Prowse to tell his old mates how well he was doing, and I grew to know Rita Gould better. Rita and her husband Ted had become for me an example of what Burt and I could do if we worked hard. Like us they had started from nothing and were building up a chain of shops. Once they asked us back to their home in Cricklewood for the weekend. It was the first time I'd ever been in an orthodox Jewish home and I was very impressed. I was beginning to realise that being Jewish was a way of life. Wherever they went they took the rules of their religion with them; it seemed to give them security.

They had a lovely house, the kind I dreamed that Burt and I might live in one day. Their two children were adorable, and Rita's old father and mother lived with them. Early in the morning I was awakened by a strange chanting.

Rita told me later with a smile, 'It's my Poppa saying his prayers. He's very orthodox.' The old man had brought his rituals, his ceremonies, his regular attendance at the synagogue with him from some far off country, and here he was in north London still with his tight Jewish world around him.

Ted Gould always made me laugh, he had that special blend of wry humour and cynicism. As spring turned into summer I discovered that he and Burt had something very much in common. They both liked horse racing.

'Doesn't Ted's gambling ever worry you?' I asked Rita.

She shrugged. 'Ted works hard, he deserves his bit of fun. But he'd never go over the edge.'

I wasn't so sure about Burt. He and Ted drove off to Ascot races in Ted's car and I found he'd put the morning's takings into his pocket. I said nothing about it, perhaps it was, as Rita said, just a bit of fun.

By the time autumn came round I knew it was more serious. Every week Burt was taking two or three days off. At first he bothered to make excuses to me saying he was off to the music publishers or some such place, but now when I saw him emptying the cash box into his pocket, I didn't even ask.

'Why is he throwing all our money away on

the horses?' I asked Rita.

'For the first time in his life Burt has money to throw away,' she said wisely. 'He'll work it out of his system, don't worry.'

I ran the shop on my own. Selling romance with my gramophone records. Dreams for the girls and boys who, on a wage of a pound a week paid one shilling and sixpence for a record about a house on a hilltop high, or a moon that shone over Kentucky. I knew I was selling them happiness in a wax disc, that they were taking these songs as their own—just as I did. When I felt blue about Burt's gambling I tried to put it out of my mind as I sang about my house on a hilltop high that I'd share with Burt.

I was twenty-one, young enough to enjoy every day as I met new people and made new friends. One of them was a very pretty girl a few years older than I. She used to come in every week to buy a new gramophone record. With her were two little girls about three and five. They looked so pretty, the three of them, in their summer dresses. One day she said, 'I've seen you having lunch in the café in the High Street. Why don't you come round to my house tomorrow and have lunch with me?'

I went to the address next day and found she was living in one of the new housing developments that were being built in Slough. It was a sparkling new house and she showed me round it proudly. She and her husband had just come back from Bathhurst in the Gambia on the West Coast of Africa where he'd been working.

She showed me photographs of the Gambia. 'Miles and miles of golden beaches,' she told me. 'We used to stand on the sands and throw out lines to catch fish. The women of the Gambia are very beautiful and wear the most gorgeous robes. Sometimes they buy so many that they bankrupt their husbands.'

We laughed together, rather pleased that there were women with such demands. Then she said, 'I wish I could be like you, have a little business of my own, go out to work and meet people. I get so lonely.'

I looked at her with amazement. She seemed to have everything a woman could desire. This lovely house, the expensive furnishings, the french windows that looked out over the fields. I'd been envying her ever since I set foot in it. And yet this girl was so lonely, that she used to walk down to the market arcade to buy a gramophone record and talk to me.

Sometimes Burt didn't even bother to come with me on the morning bus, his race meeting for the day was a train journey out of London. 'Oh it's only till the end of the flat season,' he told me. 'It's a pity to lose all these lovely days.'

What about me, I thought, I get up catch the bus to work all day at Slough and come home and cook the supper. What about me? I'll go along with it until the winter comes, I told myself, then I'll tell him, it has to stop.

'Are you building up your capital?' Rita asked me one day.

'What d'you mean?'

'Is Burt putting away money?'

I didn't know. Burt was the clever one with figures. He kept the books. He was the one who counted the takings at the end of every day. I'd been brought up like that, the man of the house held the money. Burt was the one who paid the bills to the wholesalers and the music publishers. And these bills had to be paid promptly because with the quick turnover and the new song hits coming along, we were always ordering new stock.

'I'll ask him,' I said.

'Don't do that,' said Rita, 'he'll think I'm interfering.'

It was true that when winter came Burt gave up going to the race meetings but he didn't stop betting on the horses. Street bookmaking was illegal, but Burt had only to walk to the nearest pub to find a bookie. We quarrelled about it. 'You're not suffering,' he declared, 'I pay the rent, I pay the bills.'

'But we didn't start our own business to live hand to mouth like this,' I protested. 'You're always taking money from the cashbox.'

'It's mine, isn't it,' said Burt, and because the year was 1933 and no judge had yet told a man that if his wife worked, he owed her a share, I agreed. It wasn't that Burt was mean or that he meant to be cruel but he was just damned stupid.

The man at the back of the market who re-charged the radio batteries for us made me face the truth at last. He was rather shamefaced. 'I don't like to bother you, Mrs Neighbour,' he said, 'but I need the money too and if your husband doesn't pay me . . .'

I confronted Burt. 'How many more bills haven't you paid?'

'Oh let them wait. They know they'll get their money in the end. We'll make a packet at Christmas.'

'What with?' I asked. 'If we don't pay suppliers bills they won't send us new stock.'

'Perhaps you could get a loan,' Rita advised comfortingly. 'Could your father let you have a hundred pounds to tide you over?' A hundred pounds to anyone in my family was a fortune. Even if they had it I wouldn't have borrowed it for Burt to throw away on the horses.

A debt collector from the music publisher called. Burt was out placing a bet at the pub. The man was very polite at first, but I felt instinctively that he could turn nasty. 'Unless our account is settled in seven days we may have to take court action.'

'What does that mean?'

'We shall take you to Court. Couldn't you

pay something on account?'

I was really frightened. My family had always paid their way, we had never owed money. My mother had slaved at the laundry rather than get into debt. I opened the cashbox. We'd taken twenty-two shillings and sixpence that day. I held it out to him. 'Will this do?'

Burt was very angry when he came back. 'You've cleaned us out,' he shouted. 'We haven't even got our bus fare home.'

'Let's hope you've backed a winner,' I said caustically.

The sleepless nights started. The worry because of the money we owed weighed like a millstone around my neck. When could we pay our bills off. And if we couldn't, would they send us to jail? Christmas was coming round again and there was no way we could buy the new records or the songs we needed.

Out of the blue we were resuced. A big music combine gave us an offer, they would buy us out, lock stock and barrel, just like that. They probably knew that the little music shop in the arcade could be turned into a goldmine, they also knew that we were in trouble.

We said goodbye to our friends Rita and Ted. We all smiled and joked and said better luck next time. But underneath I felt very bitter. Burt had thrown away our chance. It had been there, a chance to be somebody, to move up in the world, to have the kind of home I dreamed of, and he'd handed over everything we worked so hard for to the bookmakers.

On the bus going home that last time, I sat with the empty cashbox on my knee, a few records and copies of sheet music in a carrier bag at my feet. Burt leaned over and took my hand. We hadn't talked about it. After the first few bitter rows I'd seen that he was just as upset as I was. In spite of all his big promises that we'd try again sometime, that he'd get his old job back at Keith Prowse, I knew we were going back to the kind of life I hoped we'd escaped from, unemployment, no money, poverty . . . ! I lowered my head and for the first and last time I wept for what might have been in our little shop in the arcade.

★   ★   ★

Burt didn't go back to work at Keith Prowse. Someone else had his job and was holding on to it grimly. There were few jobs going in the Depression. Burt was much too proud to apply for assistance or ask for hand-outs, so we existed on the money he made helping shopkeepers with their income tax or keeping their books. There was no question of me going out to work for I was having a baby.

Grace, my sister, a good steady girl, who had not inherited my flights of fancy was a great help to me at this time. She was still working at

Eastman's, in a well-paid job as a dyer in the curtain department. As my confinement drew near Grace took me shopping for the baby clothes and the pram. 'Don't be silly,' she said, when I tried to thank her. 'You'd do the same for me.'

I was in labour for two days at the Park Royal Hospital. It was a difficult delivery and my son needed artifical respiration after he was born. The first person to come in and see the two of us, after Burt, was my mother. She'd had a look at my son in the nursery and asked the nurse if she could change his napkin.

'You know what, Rose,' she said beaming at me. 'Your baby had a napkin full of gold.'

'And what does that mean?'

'It means he'll be a lucky boy. First napkin change and it was a full one.'

I smiled ruefully. The last few months hadn't been very lucky trying to make one penny do the work of two.

'What are you going to call him, this lovely boy?'

'I haven't made my mind up, but it's going to be a surprise for everybody.' We smiled at each other like conspirators. We both knew that Burt's mother, my mother-in-law, had plans that must be thwarted.

She came in to see me, Burt's mother. She was wearing a new hat, Sherwood green it was called, with a tall feather at the side like Robin

Hood. I couldn't take my eyes off it. She admired the baby and said he looked just like his father, although Burt of course had more colour in his cheeks, then she folded her hands in her lap and said. 'I've told you Rose, that it's a tradition in our family to give the first boy the family names.' She rolled them off her tongue with relish, 'Albert, William, Joseph'.

I'd heard it before but I was still appalled. That the poor little mite lying at my side should be saddled with that mouthful, that my mother-in-law should tell me what to call my baby. What cheek! I glanced down at the copy of *Picturegoer* lying on my bed. On the cover, smiling up at me was one of the most handsome of British film stars: Brian Aherne. He had fair hair well brushed back and a thin moustache that reminded me of Burt's.

I eyed the feather in her hat. 'What a pity,' I said, 'but we've decided that our son shall only have one name. It'll be easier for him.'

My mother-in-law looked very put out, but she tried to make the best of things. 'All right. Which one is it going to be, Albert, William or Joseph?'

Before I answered I turned the copy of *Picturegoer* face down, no sense in looking for trouble. 'We've chosen a lovely name?' I said, making up my mind quite quickly and quite definitely. 'It's Brian!' and to myself I added 'Thanks to Mr Aherne.'

*   *   *

Just as my mother said baby Brian did take home a napkin full of gold. On the first Saturday after we came back from the hospital Burt won fifty pounds on the football pools. Instant riches! Oh, all right, he was gambling, but so was almost every working man in England. They all did the football pools. And for us it meant for a time an end of scraping and making do. There wasn't a happier new Mum and Dad in Acton.

By the time Brian was six months old Burt still hadn't found a job. It wasn't his fault. There just weren't enough jobs around in Jubilee Year, 1935. He wasn't the kind of man who liked to sit at home so most days he'd go down to the Billiard Hall and play snooker. That was when I started walking. After I'd finished my housework I'd put Brian in his pram and walk. I think I walked all over London. Sometimes Aunt Rose would come with me and we'd walk to Hyde Park Corner and sit in the Park or go down to the Serpentine. I never had a penny in my pocket and I felt quite frustrated. I was young and I wanted some of the pretty things I saw in the shop windows in Oxford Street. I looked in Hamley's windows in Regent Street and longed to go in and buy a toy for my baby. One day I decided that I'd had enough of stewing up bones and barley for supper.

I went round to see my mother. 'If I got some kind of part-time work would you look after Brian for me, Mum? He's a very good baby and never cries once you put him down.'

My mother knew Burt's character well. 'He'll never stand for you working, Rose.'

'Why not?' I demanded. 'I can't go on like this month after month and never a penny to my name. After all, Mum, you went back to the laundry when Dad was out of work.'

'Times were different, and your father was different.' I knew she meant that Dad had never spent his time down at the Billiard Hall.

'It would only mean a few hours a week, evening work. I have to do something, Mum.' I pleaded, 'It's awful living this kind of life.'

My mother knew me well. 'You've found a job already, haven't you?'

I'd found a job as an usherette at the Globe Cinema. The cinema where not so long ago Peggy and I had entered for our first Talent Contest. Burt hated me working. He hated the smart black uniform and high heeled shoes I wore and the admiring glances of some of my male customers. Every evening for three hours I could leave the kitchen sink and the suet puddings and the scrag ends of lamb, join a make believe world where James Cagney was Public Enemy Number One and Sylvia Sidney and Henry Fonda went down the Trail of the Lonesome Pine.

At the back of my mind was the hope that my job would prove to be the pressure that would make Burt find a job, but it wasn't until Janet Gaynor and Marlene Dietrich appeared on the scene that anything happened.

Gaumont British gave a day's outing to any member of their staff who liked a picnic. The Manager of the Globe suggested that Sally, another usherette at the cinema, and I might like to go. 'You've got to be young and healthy for that kind of lark,' he said. 'You two ought to look all right in fancy dress.'

There was to be a special contest for the employees who could best impersonate the famous film stars of the day. It was right up my street.

Burt said, no, his wife wasn't going to show her legs to that crowd of gaping men. 'Mum,' I said to my closest ally, 'I want to go. Sally and I have worked out costumes that won't cost a penny. We might even win.'

'You go, Rose,' she told me. 'You're only young once, and all the good times end too quickly. I'll look after Brian and Burt can come here for his dinner.'

A special bus picked up Sally and me outside Acton tube station and we spent the day, along with hundreds of other employees of Gaumont British at their Morden sports ground. It was a great occasion and the high spot came in the afternoon with the film star parade. We changed into our costumes with the rest of the girls. Sally, who had curly red hair, a tiny dimple in the chin and big brown eyes looked the image of Janet Gaynor. She had on the kind of ragged cotton dress the star had worn in *Seventh Heaven*. I was much more sophisticated in black fishnet tights, high heeled shoes, scanty black shorts, a white satin blouse and a black top hat. I twirled an ebony cane and with my blonde hair and carefully applied make-up, I felt that I had just stepped out of the Blue Angel night club.

We paraded in front of the judges, the imitation Joan Crawfords, Greta Garbos and Jean Harlows. Some of the judges were well-known film stars themselves. When the parade was over we stood in a nervous group waiting for the results.

'The first prize,' came the clear voice over the loudspeaker 'is for a young lady from the Globe Cinema, Acton.' We all held our breaths . . . 'Janet Gaynor!'

When the cheers died down, we heard, 'And the winner of the second prize is also a young lady from the Globe Cinema. Marlene Dietrich.'

I'd won. Second prize was just as good.

Much later an elated Marlene Dietrich went home with her second prize, a white leather fitted vanity case. Success had gone to my head. I didn't give a damn what Burt said. He was sitting in his armchair studiously reading the paper and ignoring me. I could see by the set of his chin that inside he was doing a slow burn. I steeled myself for the explosion.

'Look what I've won,' I said nonchalantly, laying the vanity case on the table.

Burt put down his paper and grunted something.

'Won't they be surprised at the Globe?' I was feeling slightly less certain of myself.

Burt stood up. 'And I've got another surprise for the manager at the Globe.' His voice rose. 'Tell him you're leaving!'

My mouth dropped open. 'Oh, no!'

'I've got a job. A permanent job. Costing Clerk at Deacons the builders.'

We looked at each other. In his eyes, just for a second, I glimpsed something unsure. Burt was never very good at playing the masterful male. He needed help. I smiled and capitulated, 'Does that mean I'm going to be a lady of leisure again?'

'That's about it.' He nodded at the vanity case on the table, 'You can sit at home and do your face up all day long.'

We both started to laugh. It was the best kind of ending to a lovely day

★　　　★　　　★

It wasn't at all bad being a full-time housewife again, now that I had some housekeeping to spend. But things still went wrong. Out of the blue a letter arrived. Notice to quit our flat in Berrymead Gardens. And we had no idea why. The rent of £1 a week, no matter how difficult to find, was always paid on the dot. Burt was wrapped up in his new job, I didn't want to worry him, so I went round to see my father.

'Dan Ryder,' said my father, 'the poor man's lawyer. Go and see him.'

Dan Ryder, who lived in Chiswick was a solicitor in his fifties. He was politically minded and used to sit in the public gallery of the House of Commons, listening to the debates. Either because of his politics or because of the kindness of his heart, he helped the poor who couldn't afford legal fees.

'Go to Acton Town Hall, Mrs Neighbour,' he told me, 'and find out if this property has been registered as de-controlled. If it hasn't then I can help you.'

I went along to the Town Hall. The property had not been de-controlled. Under Mr Ryder's instructions I sent this information to the landlord and made a copy of my letter.

'Sit tight,' was his next advice. 'They can't evict you even if they threaten to send in the bailiffs.'

The landlord did write us a letter threatening

us with the bailiffs, he did refuse to take rent from us, and in spite of Dan Ryder's assurances, we were very worried. Every week I put the rent in the post office savings bank, for I was sure that the day of reckoning would arrive sooner or later.

'Now take all these letters and copies of your replies to Mr Levy, a solicitor in Fulham,' ordered Dan Ryder. 'He will charge you one guinea and then your troubles will be over.'

In due course we had a letter from Mr Levy to say that the real rent of our flat in Berrymead Gardens should be twelve shillings not one pound, so that not only did the landlord owe us money but we were quite safe. He could not evict us.

I learned a good lesson from Dan Ryder. How to write letters to those in authority, how not to be browbeaten by them, and how to fight for what I thought was right.

One Sunday morning in 1937 I was busy cooking in the kitchen. I wanted to get the dinner early for Burt was playing cricket in the afternoon and I was taking Brian along for the outing.

Someone tapped on the scullery door then pushed it open. My father's head came round.

'Hallo, Dad,' I said, 'did you miss Burt, he took Brian round to see you?' I closed the oven door and straightened up. There was something about him, a tight worried look on his face. 'Is anything wrong?' I asked anxiously.

'Come and sit down and I'll tell you.'

'What is it?' I clung to his arm. 'It's not Brian. Nothing's happened to Brian.'

He led me to the table. We sat down next to the starched white tablecloth laid for the big meal of the week. 'It's not Brian, It's Burt. He's had a haemorrhage, a bad one. I called an ambulance straight away and they've taken him to the Central Middlesex Hospital.'

CHAPTER SIX

THERE MUST BE MORE TO MARRIAGE THAN MISERY

Burt wasn't dead or dying when I arrived at the hospital. He was sitting up in bed looking very sorry for himself. 'We'll keep him in bed for a few days,' said the house surgeon, 'and do a few tests. Has he had TB?'

I shook my head. Neither of us were ever ill.

Burt had the tests and X-rays to decide whether the trouble lay in his lungs or his stomach. But as far as I could see, no one seemed to find out. 'Watch him carefully,' ordered the hospital when he was discharged and we went home in a taxi.

For the first few days I watched Burt with as

much dread as if he was a bomb about to explode. I sat bolt upright next to him in bed every night, in case he should lapse into a coma or start bleeding. I crept out of bed with black circles under my eyes and Burt slept on as peacefully as a baby. He ate well, he slept well, but Burt's whole foundations had been shaken by his haemorrhage. He took on invalid status.

Our doctor who called in to see him daily was a kind, slow moving Irishman. He was a great believer in tender, loving care. 'Let the boy have a good rest in bed, that's the ticket.' The days turned into weeks and after a month Burt finally got up and sat in an armchair with a blanket over his knees worrying about his health. We were back where we had started from. Broke!

'When will he be fit enough to go back to work?' I asked the doctor.

'Ah, that we cannot tell.'

With Burt's mysterious malady keeping him fully occupied there was only one thing for me to do. Find a job, earn some money and buy the food.

I found a job in the lower echelons of the musical world. Winding coils for radiograms at EMI. My new routine was to get up at six, take Brian down to my mother's, catch a bus to Ealing Common, then take another bus to Hayes, Middlesex to the EMI Factory. At six in the evening I'd pick up Brian and go home,

101

cook the supper and do the housework.'

Burt left on his own was improving, he soon found the strength to get down to the Billiard Hall for a game of snooker.

'Are you strong enough to wash up the breakfast dishes and light the fire?' I asked him.

He sighed. He was one of the old school who thought that housework was not for men. 'I'll try.'

After six months of this, I was not only tired out, I was growing angry at coming home to a dirty flat every evening. None of my threats to give up work if he didn't help in the house did any good. Burt took his pilgrimage to the doctor's surgery every week to pick up his bottle of tonic. He was still on the panel, so I decided to call on the doctor myself.

'No, I can't find anything physically wrong with him Mrs Neighbour, it's his nerves.'

'Isn't there any medicine for nerves?'

The doctor shook his head doubtfully. 'Thousands of people are walking around with nervous debility. You know it's a bit like shell shock. Takes people in odd ways.' The doctor showed me out and gave me a reassuring pat on the back. 'One of these days he'll be his old self again. Just be patient. Let's leave it in the good Lord's hands.'

On Monday morning the alarm clock went off at six. Burt shook my shoulder, 'That's the alarm Rose. You'd better get up.'

I was wide awake ready to give Burt's shell shock a bit of my own treatment. 'I've given up work, Burt. I'm going to have a nice lie in this morning.'

'But you can't Rose, we need the money.'

I yawned happily, as I remembered the reassuring words of the doctor.

'Don't worry Burt,' I said sweetly, 'the Good Lord will provide.'

Throughout the morning Burt behaved like a hunted animal. He couldn't even read the *Sporting Life* in peace as I harried him from pillar to post, scrubbing, sweeping, giving the living room a well needed spring clean. In two days Burt had completely recovered his health. My father found him a job at Napier's, where he worked himself, and from that day onwards Burt never mentioned his mysterious illness again.

Strangely enough it was at Napier's, the aero engine factory that Burt found his right niche doing a job that gave him great satisfaction. There wasn't much doubt that war was approaching and Burt who was an expert costing clerk was moved into a top secret department. New planes were on the drawing board, new experiments with jet engines and Burt's talent for figures was just right for working out the cost of these wonder machines.

I was happy that Burt was doing so well but I was also worried. When Burt had money in his pocket it always found its way into the bookmakers' hands. I soon found out that he was gambling again, but I told myself that as long as I had my housekeeping I should leave well alone.

1937 was the year Grace, my sister, married René Vignon. She met a young Frenchman while walking in Gunnersbury Park with a girlfriend. One Sunday she brought him home for tea. 'He looks just like Errol Flynn,' I whispered to my mother.

'Doesn't act very foreign, though, does he?'

René had quite a romantic background. He'd been brought up in a much more prosperous atmosphere than ours. His father had died when he was a baby and his mother, a Parisienne, had sent him to live with her parents who ran a French hotel in Russell Square.

Although his grandmother had lived in London for forty years she spoke not a word of English. 'She used to mock my French accent,' René told us. 'She gave me a complex about it, so when she spoke to me in French I always answered in English.' Because they were so busy his grandparents employed a nanny to look after him, and when his mother came over from Paris to see him, he was scared of the beautiful stranger and always whispered to his nanny about 'that lady'.

René must have had a lonely childhood living

in a French household in central London. 'I was a bit of a loner,' he said. 'Not sure what I was.' When he met Grace, for the first time in his life he felt the warmth of a close-knit family. My parents had little money but their home was filled with love and René took to Petersfield Road and my Mum and Dad like a duck to water. He wanted nothing better than to marry Grace and become part of Soap Suds Island.

'René,' said my mother, that first afternoon. 'What a mouthful! Shall we call you Ronnie?'

'But if there's a war, Ronnie?' my father asked him, 'Which country will you fight for, England or France?'

'England,' said Ronnie, 'Grace and I will be British.'

We asked endless questions about René's background. Why his mother had always relinquished him finally to her own mother, every time she took her son back to Paris with her. What was Paris like? What was his mother like? His life had a foreign touch that intrigued us all.

What René didn't tell us was that he was heir to a considerable fortune. His godmother, a Baroness, an aristocratic lady from the Bourbon Parma family had looked after his welfare when his grandparents died. She was a wealthy widow and lived alone in a large house in Russell Square. When the Baroness died her fortune was to be divided between René and her other godson who lived in France.

Even if she had known, it wouldn't have made any difference to Grace. She loved Ronnie for himself and they were going to live the kind of life they both wanted. They'd found themselves a flat in Clovely Road just round the corner from Petersfield Road, so that Grace could call in and see her mother every day. Ronnie might be rich one day but at the moment they were just an ordinary young couple preparing their new home in Acton.

Ronnie's mother came over from Paris for the wedding. Her name was Antoinette and she and Grace loved each other from the moment they met. Antoinette was very slim and elegant with large dark eyes and a sweet smile. With her came Ronnie's godmother, the Baroness, a real society lady. These two Frenchwomen in their beautiful clothes brought a Parisien chic to St Mary's Church, Acton, that really made heads turn. Antoinette, I remember, had her hair swept up under a little hat covered in roses. Edwardian styles were coming into vogue in 1937, full skirts, crinoline dresses in the evening, as though the fashion dictators knew there was a war coming and they wanted the women of Europe to wear pretty frocks in the short time that was left to them.

All the family were there, Aunt Rose and Uncle Dick who now lived in Acton Lane, Edna their daughter who had just married a nice young man called Harry. Aunt Alice and her family, and all the Aunts and Uncles from my father's side. That evening when it was over, I put the big black kettle on my mother's hob and looked up at the wistful face of the picture on the wall. 'You should have been here, Aunt Agnes,' I said to her, 'it was a lovely day. Little Grace has married a Frenchman.'

★　　　★　　　★

Just before eleven o'clock on Sunday morning of September 3, 1939, I placed the rice pudding I had just prepared in the oven, lit the gas, then went to sit with Grace in the living room. Brian, aged five sat on her knee, eyes round with excitement, he knew from the atmosphere around him that something was about to happen. At eleven o'clock precisely Neville Chamberlain, the Prime Minister of Great Britain, announced over the radio that we were now at war with Germany.

Because Grace and I could hardly remember the 1918 war we were both filled with strange emotions. Fear wasn't one of them for we hadn't the faintest idea of what this war was going to be like. There'd been all this talk of bombs; we'd collected gas masks from the Town Hall, people were building Anderson bomb shelters in their back gardens, but it all seemed unreal. In fact we both felt rather excited.

Suddenly we knew there really was a war on. The ghastly banshee wail of an air raid siren came flooding through the open windows. About two minutes later the scullery door burst open and my father charged in.

'Girls! Girls,' he shouted, 'come on down to the shelter, that's the air raid warning.'

Grace wasn't very nimble, she was pregnant with her first baby, but we hurried out and were treated to our first laugh of the war. There was the air raid warden with his tin hat on running in front of us shouting, 'Follow me!' He turned round to make sure we were and ran full tilt into a lamp post. The noise was terrific as his tin hat struck iron.

In the public shelter were all the family, the Uncles, the Aunts, and the neighbours looking very surprised at being rushed out of the pubs and the kitchens at a moment's notice. The All Clear sounded very soon. I believe it was an enemy aircraft over London, but it didn't drop any bombs.

'That's it,' said my father as soon as we were back home in Petersfield Road. 'You two girls have got to be evacuated. What with Grace's condition and Rose and her little boy, Acton won't be safe. It's an enemy target and they're sure to drop bombs on Napier's aircraft factory. Go and get your bags packed and I'll take you down to the Evacuation Centre.'

The Evacuation Centre at Acton was fairly humming with activity. Pregnant women lumbered around, small children wailed as labels were pinned to their coats. 'I'm not sure about this,' I said to Grace, as my father organised our departure.

'Neither am I,' said Grace. 'Let's go home.'

At that moment a large lady herded us into a bus and there was no escape. After dark the bus arrived in Dorchester, the county town of Dorset. An interminable wait and then the flickering torches of the ladies of the Evacuee Committee (those who hadn't gone to bed) picked us out in the black-out. Someone agreed to take us over, and feeling that we'd just arrived on the slave ship from Africa, Grace and I, and a very sleepy Brian, trotted after her. The first householder had locked up and gone to bed and the awful thought occurred to me that maybe no one wanted to take us in. Why, oh why, had we come?

Fortunately the second door our leader banged on was opened to us. A kindly-faced woman in a dressing gown gave us cups of tea and ham sandwiches and showed us to a very large bed, big enough for the three of us.

Grace and I lay in bed together holding hands just as we used to when we were little girls. 'I suppose you can't blame them,' I murmured, 'I think they only get five bob a week for each of us. You know it's a good thing we're on the small side, else they might have hired us out as farm labourers.'

Grace whispered unhappily, 'I hope Ronnie got some supper.'

I sat up, 'Oh my goodness, I've just remembered! I left a rice pudding in the oven and forgot to turn off the gas. Poor old Burt.'

For the second time on the day war broke out we both rocked with laughter at the misfortunes of others.

A letter arrived from my father. He'd decided that it was going to be a long war, so we'd better dig in and make the best of it. 'Go for trips down to the sea-side,' he wrote. My mother added a postscript. 'Rose, you forgot to turn off the gas. I had to throw the pudding dish into the dustbin.'

We did try to make the best of Dorchester, and we took trips down to Weymouth and gazed out at the English Channel. Not much was going on, the pierrots had left, the cinemas were closed and there were a lot of cheeky young sailors about. We let Brian have a paddle and we sat in deck chairs longing for Petersfield Road, Mum and Dad, the Aunts and Uncles, and of course our husbands.

Grace missed Ronnie a great deal. They had just come back from a trip to Paris where they had stayed with Antoinette and Grace was now wearing the latest Paris styles. She looked extra smart on the afternoon we tried to book her into a nursing home, and her tip tilted hat with a snood was the latest fashion.

If, as my father declared, it was going to be a long war, we decided that Grace should book a bed for her confinement. The nursing home was up a long drive behind tall trees and as soon as we crossed the threshold and saw the starched uniforms of the nurses in the cathedral gloom of the polished hall, we began to wonder.

The matron interviewed us in her office. 'Quite impossible,' she announced. 'We have enough to do looking after our *own* people.' Although she didn't add 'without being bothered by you unwanted evacuees', it was implied just the same.

'But what shall I do?' faltered Grace.

The matron shrugged her shoulders. 'I can only suggest the Infirmary.'

'The Infirmary!' we both exclaimed.

'Yes, it used to be the workhouse.'

We went straight back and packed our suitcase. We were on the next train to London. As the train drew out of the station we felt like thumbing our noses at Dorchester. The workhouse! What cheek!

★　　　★　　　★

Burt wasn't called up because his job at Napier's was top priority. He was working with the new Sabre jets. He also did two nights a week with the Home Guard keeping watch over Napier's factory.

Ronnie joined the Fire Service and in the winter of 1940 he was one of the men who stopped London being burned down. He saw terrible sights, digging mothers and their babies out from under the staircases where they had sheltered. The sight of so much carnage filled him with fear that his little daughter Marianne and Grace might one day be killed by the Nazi bombs. 'You've just got to be evacuated,' he told Grace and me. 'One day it might be you and the children I have to dig out.'

This time we went to Ron's friends who had a farm near Totnes in Devon. We had an absolutely lovely time, but after a couple of months we were homesick again and wanted to change the green hills of Devon for the grey streets of Acton. 'We're cockney sparrows,' I told Grace. 'I can't leave London.'

When we arrived home, however, I did understand that it wasn't fair to keep Brian in Acton which was being pounded in the bombing. So we moved to the outskirts of London, to a suburb called Southall ten miles outside London and half an hour's bus ride from Acton. Southall, so far, was free of bombing and the maisonette flat we found was very nice. Unfortunately Brian hated the move and his new school. He'd been happy in Acton with all his friends and his grandparents round the corner and he found it hard to settle down in Southall.

Looking back, the move to Southall brought problems for the three of us. That was the time I discovered that my engagement ring was missing. At first I was horrified, then I told myself that no one could have broken into the flat and only one person could have taken it.

'Burt,' I said, when he came home that evening, 'I want my engagement ring back.'

At first I thought he was going to deny it, then he said rather shamefaced, 'I needed some ready money so I borrowed it. Don't worry you'll get it back.' I didn't. I never saw my ring again.

A week later I saw that my watch had gone. 'You know where it is, Rose,' I told myself, 'at the pawnshop in Acton.' The same thing began to happen to many things in our little flat. One by one the wedding presents disappeared, a little silver vase, a cut glass bowl. We began to quarrel. It seemed so stupid to me that even in the worst days when we hadn't a penny to bless ourselves with, we hadn't gone down to the pawnshop. And now when he had a good job and was earning good money, the home we had kept together at such pains was being frittered away to the bookmakers.

I knew perfectly well what was happening. Burt was putting every penny he could lay his hands on to the horses for that lucky win that would solve all his problems. When the Turkey red carpet from the living room was rolled up one early morning and taken away, I went over to Acton to see my father.

'Burt is doing very well at Napier's,' my father told me, 'there shouldn't be any financial problems. But I'll ask around on the quiet and try and find out what the trouble is.'

Just as I thought, my father found out that Burt owed a lot of money to the bookmaker who was always on hand on the shop floor at Napier's. Although it was illegal, there was usually a bookie in every factory.

'Is he giving you any housekeeping?' my father asked.

'Not very much,' I had to admit. As so often happened, before I left to catch the bus back to Southall my parents lent me money. Grace also used to lend me money. And I felt so humiliated that I had to accept it for Brian's sake.

I don't know which is worst, to be married to an alcoholic or a compulsive gambler. They are both heart-breaking experiences. But at least it shows when your husband is drunk, unlike the gambler who puts your last penny on the horses and doesn't tell you until there's no money to pay the rent. I felt so angry and helpless at this flaw in Burt's character. He was a kind man, he wouldn't normally hurt anyone, but now if he needed money to put on the horses, nothing

114

seemed to stop him getting it. Our home could be sold up, we could be out on the streets, and he wouldn't or couldn't fight this terrible addiction.

I'd made a new friend in Southall, my next door neighbour, a pretty Irish girl called Maureen. She came from a farm outside Dublin and her Irish brogue was a joy to listen to, 'Men!' she said, when I told her of my troubles with Burt, 'I can't say I have a very high opinion of them meself.' Her husband, Charlie, was away with the Merchant Navy, keeping the sea routes open, and she only saw him when he came home on leave.

Every Saturday Burt and I used to have an evening out. Brian stayed with my mother and we sometimes went to the cinema, visited relatives or even went dancing. One Saturday Burt said to me, 'There's a snooker match at the Billiard Hall in Acton, d'you mind if we don't go out together?'

I thought he looked very smart for a game of snooker when he left that Saturday evening, I must admit that my female intuition did have a twinge or two, but I didn't want to start a quarrel. A week or two later he told me that there was a staff dance at Napier's, unfortunately for employees only, and he added the usual words, 'you don't mind if I go, do you?'

My father, quite innocently let the cat out of

the bag, when I was over visiting my parents. 'Going to the dance on Saturday, Rose?' he asked.

'I can't, it's for employees only.' My mother and father exchanged a look. 'Well, isn't it?' I asked.

'I think Burt may have got it wrong.'

'All right Dad,' I said, catching on very quickly, 'if wives can go, how about getting a couple of tickets for me and a friend.'

Maureen was very willing to accompany me. We were both curious to know what Burt was up to. As soon as Burt, dressed up to the nines, hair shining with Brylcreem, had left for the dance, it was off with my pinafore, on with my dance dress and a race with Maureen to catch the bus to Acton.

The dance at Napier's, held in the canteen, was in full swing when we arrived. We settled ourselves in a quiet corner and watched the dancers. Right in the middle of the throng was a tall debonair man and a tall dark woman. They danced well together and when the music stopped Burt put his arm around his partner's waist to lead her back to their table. It took me back to the days at Kew Palais de Danse when Burt and Ivy had made such an elegant couple.

'Not a care in the world, that husband of yours,' said Maureen. 'Men!' I watched them with a sick feeling in my stomach. How could he bend his head, smile at this woman, laugh at

116

her little jokes? Burt got up to make his way over to the bar to get fresh drinks. Something made him look across to our corner. I saw his jaw drop, the apprehension on his face, then he recovered himself and waved to me. We looked at each other across a crowded room and whatever enchantment was left after ten years of marriage quickly disintegrated. To me Burt was like a stranger. He'd been looking at another woman the way he used to look at me. In spite of all the hard times, all the anxiety over the gambling, the unpaid bills, the broken promises, I had never seriously thought of leaving him until now. He was my husband and I had to take the rough with the smooth, just as my mother and her generation had always done.

'Fancy seeing you here,' said Burt when he came over to our table. For all the concern he showed I might have been a casual acquaintance.

I smiled at him. Maureen smiled at him. And my heart was pounding so heavily that I thought he'd hear it.

'I'm with friends,' Burt explained, 'colleages from the office.'

'And the dark haired colleague,' I enquired, 'the one you've been dancing with?'

'Oh, that's Cynthia.'

We continued to smile at each other. 'We're with friends too,' I waved airily towards the group of men on the fringe of the dance floor.

117

'Oh, then you're all right.' He actually sounded relieved.

We weren't with friends, but we soon found some. I danced and laughed and chatted, and inside I felt ready to explode. At eleven o'clock I sauntered across the dance floor and said to Burt, 'Well, I'm off now.' My eyes rested on Cynthia, but her face was just a white blob to me, I was so angry and upset.

'See you later then,' said Burt happily.

'Did you hear what he said?' I asked Maureen once we were outside. *'See you later!!* Who does he think I am? His maiden aunt?'

'That fella has the cheek of the devil,' Maureen agreed.

'This is it!' I announced dramatically. 'The straw that finally broke the camel's back. I shall leave him.'

'Ah, don't be saying that,' Maureen tried to calm me down. 'You can't leave a man just because he goes out dancing.'

I spent that night at my mother's house in Acton where I'd left Brian in the afternoon. On Sunday morning I caught the bus home and Burt and I were reunited over the breakfast table. 'That was a fine thing!' I said as an opening shot.

Burt wore an injured expression. 'You didn't have to go off to your mother's like that.'

'You mean I should have stayed with you, then we could both have taken Cynthia home?'

'Cynthia,' said Burt severely, 'is a colleague at work'.

*   *   *

Shortly afterwards I was opening the morning post and there was this letter addressed to Burt in a pale blue envelope. I always opened all the letters no matter to whom they were addressed; if Burt was down first, he did the same. This particular letter was from Burt's colleague, the one called Cynthia, telling him that she'd love to go dog racing and she'd meet him outside the Stadium next Saturday evening.

I left it on the table next to his toast and marmalade. 'It's from that colleague of yours,' I said, slamming down the tea-pot and scalding myself. 'It seems that she wants you to do some overtime.'

Burt denied everything. He was innocent. Cynthia was innocent. I was the one with the suspicious mind. If a man couldn't go dancing and dog racing with a friend from the office? But if I was so abnormally jealous he'd have to explain to Cynthia. Did I want that, he demanded?

'Yes, I do,' I shouted, 'and while you're telling her that you won't be seeing her any more, I'd like you to add a few details.' The details would have filled a book.

The quarrels never seemed to stop. I didn't

trust him any more. If he was late coming home from work I suspected the worst. If Burt gambled and lost the housekeeping money, I didn't accept his usual excuses with a sigh, I told him just how much I despised him. We agreed on nothing except that we should never quarrel in front of Brian. That made it even harder for we had to bottle up our resentment until Brian was either in bed or out of the flat. Brian who hated being evacuated to Southall because of the bombs had no idea that another war had broken out between his two parents.

Maureen, my Irish friend was a great help during this time. I needed someone to confide in, for I couldn't tell my family. She listened to me, supported me and thanked her lucky stars that Charlie her husband was away at sea, far from the wiles of other women.

We both agreed that some strange revolution was taking place between the once happily married couples of Great Britain. Men were being uprooted from their home environment, women were being sent to work in factories. It wasn't just the fighting men overseas who were finding a new kind of freedom; the women they left behind, and the men who remained in Britain, were changing. The old-fashioned values seemed to be on the way out and there was a new kind of sexual liberty.

Neither Maureen nor I wanted any part of it but it was being forced upon us. Even Maureen was caught up in it. She and Charlie had been childhood sweethearts. 'He could hardly see across the room for the smoke of my mother's turf fire,' she told me, 'but there he sat night after night until I agreed to marry him.' When he came home on leave she was radiant with happiness. And then there came an urgent telegram from Dublin to say her mother was ill and would she come over?

'If you'd just look in on the poor boy now and then,' she asked me. 'Buy his rations for him, for he doesn't know a thing about looking after himself.'

She gave me Charlie's ration book and a key to the front door and I promised to look after him like a mother. I didn't know that the last thing Charlie wanted was a mother. Filled with neighbourly zeal I shopped for Charlie, made him a shepherd's pie and went next door. It was about twelve midday so I guessed he'd be down at the pub. Just as I thought the kitchen needed tidying up and then I decided to make the bed for the poor neglected boy. With the carpet sweeper in one hand and a duster in the other I opened the bedroom door. I blinked once or twice to make sure I wasn't seeing things. Charlie was curled up in the double bed and there nestling by him, her red hair making a nice splash of colour on the pillow, was a strange woman. They were both sound asleep.

I went straight home, made a cup of tea and

sat down at the kitchen table to drink it. Maybe I had a suspicious mind as Burt was always pointing out. Maybe the strange female was just a friend who needed a bed for the night. A colleague, perhaps? 'If you believe that, Rose Neighbour,' I said to myself, 'you'll believe anything.'

I was still trying to work it out when my doorbell rang. A raving lunatic stood outside, a lunatic with an Irish brogue. 'The dirty bastard,' he yelled, 'he's got that slut of a barmaid from the Bull's Head in there with him, and me poor sister over in Dublin with me poor sick mother.'

Curtains began to twitch, doors began to open, 'Come in,' I said hastily. 'Let's talk about it inside, maybe it's only friendship.'

'There is no such thing as friendship between a married man and another woman,' shouted the Irish lunatic, who was Maureen's brother, and also had a key to the maisonette. Maureen had been very liberal with her keys.

Nothing would satisfy him but that a telegram be sent to Maureen asking her to return at once. The disaster on her doorstep was more important than her poor sick mother. Maureen and I commiserated together when she returned. 'We don't deserve it, Rose,' she wept. 'We've never looked at another man, and those devils of husbands sleeping around like tomcats. And mine in me own bed, in the linen sheets Aunt Bernadette gave us for a wedding present.'

For two days while she scrubbed the maisonette out with lysol she spoke not a word to Charlie. But then her brother made them both go down to the priest. Charlie confessed all—he'd have been hard put to deny it—and said he'd never commit such a terrible sin again. The priest gave him a lecture on the sanctity of marriage patted him on the shoulder and told Maureen to forgive him.

Although she and Charlie kissed and made up the thought of the other woman in her bed still rankled. 'What did you say was the name of that pub, Rose?' she asked. 'Will we pay that barmaid a visit one evening?'

Neither of us drank, neither of us had ever been in a pub without our husbands so it was quite an ordeal going up to the bar behind which the red headed woman stood polishing glasses. There was no mistaking that hennaed hair. 'What can I do for you?' she asked, giving us a contemptuous look.

I felt Maureen next to me start to tremble, her voice came out in a high squeak. 'I want to have a word with you and I'm after asking you to come outside.' The woman went on polishing the glass in her hand. She blew on it, gave it an extra shine and said nothing.

'It's about me husband,' Maureen said unsteadily but she kept talking.

'I don't care who your husband is. I'm not coming outside.'

'Oh yes you are,' I chimed in, 'or I'll fetch the manager.'

A certain amount of interest was now being shown, one or two people looked our way.

'You'll do no such thing,' said the woman. Then, deciding that perhaps we could become a nuisance, she laid down her glass. 'I'll give you two minutes,' she offered angrily. 'Wait for me outside.'

In the forecourt of the pub Maureen started to talk quite reasonably, telling her how Charlie had always been a good husband . . . how shocked she had been to discover he'd been unfaithful to her . . .

'You make me sick,' interrupted the red haired woman. 'Look, if you can't hold your husband that's your fault. Don't come whining to me.'

'Rose,' shouted Maureen, 'Get her arms.'

I was just as surprised as the red head, but quick as a flash. I slipped behind her and held her while Maureen lifted her hand and gave her a resounding slap on the face. The lights of a bus passing the forecourt interrupted us. We both turned and ran like hell after it. We caught it, just as the conductor rang his bell. We didn't care where it was going as long as it took us away from the red head—fast. We went all the way to Hounslow giggling like a pair of schoolgirls.

At last we'd delivered a blow for long-suffering wives.

Maureen's trouble unsettled me. Engrained into my very being were the old-fashioned notions of my parent's generation. A woman should put up with her husband, she must keep the home together because of the children. A woman who left her husband would lead an isolated life filled with money worries, she would lose her status, lose everything that made life worth living. Was this really true, I asked myself? Would Brian suffer without his father? As he grew older he must find out that his father was a chronic gambler. Finally, there was my increasing worry, had Brian inherited the terrible flaw of compulsive gambling, just as Burt had from his father?

For the past year Burt and I had put up with a great deal of emotional battering from each other. Every time he came home late I suspected the worst, every time I accused him he attacked me verbally. Although Brian did not hear our quarrels, the sight of a tight-lipped mother and a scowling father wasn't a good image for a child to grow up with. My childhood had been so happy. I had never heard my parents' voices raised against each other. I felt that Burt and I were failing our son. Would the scars of his parents' quarrels mark him for life?

We went through another bad period of losing money to the bookmakers and now we quarrelled about money. All I had in my purse was two shillings. That evening I asked him for money to buy the food next day. 'What can I do with two shillings?' I asked angrily.

Burt got up from the table. He didn't bother to reply. He collected his equipment for the Home Guard, it was one of his nights on duty, and left the house. I started to clear away the supper things. So this is marriage I thought to myself, sheer bitter unhappiness. I was turning into a shrew and Burt was becoming an insensitive bully. We were bad for each other. He would never give up gambling and I would never accept it. We were tearing each other to pieces with our constant quarrels.

'What can I do with the two shillings?' I'd cried. Well there was something I could do. I could catch a bus and leave. I went into Brian's room. He was lying face down on his bed reading a comic, his head propped up on his elbows.

'Put your shoes on Brian,' I said. 'We're going out.'

There must be a better life than this somewhere, I thought. Was it selfish to want to be happy? Yet, could I survive without a husband, could I bring up a child alone? I'll have a damn good try, I decided. Ten minutes later, I slammed the front door behind me and I never, ever, went back.

CHAPTER SEVEN

MY LOVE WORE AN AMERICAN UNIFORM

Maureen answered the phone. 'I've left Burt,' I said, 'and I'm in Piccadilly tube station.'

'Are you now!' She hesitated as if she couldn't quite understand what I was doing down there. 'When are you coming home?'

'I'm not coming back to Southall. Brian's staying with my mother in Acton.'

To give Maureen her due, she now grasped the situation immediately. 'So you want me to get your things, is that it?'

'Yes, please.' We'd always had keys to each other's homes.

'And where d'you think you are going to live now?'

'That's one of my problems.'

'Tell you what you can do,' said Maureen. 'move in with Tommy. You know Tommy, she's my friend Lilian the hairdresser. She's got this great big house in Harrow full of empty bedrooms. She'd welcome you. And the poor girl's all alone with that husband of hers away in the Forces.'

Lilian was nick-named Tommy because she'd trained to be a hairdresser by first cutting men's hair in a barber's shop in Harrow and had married another hairdresser. But she'd given up her shop when she became pregnant and her husband joined the army.

As soon as I rang her doorbell and saw her, I liked Tommy. She was pretty with a head of short blonde curls, dimples and twinkling blue eyes. And she was pleased to have me share her house for she was very pregnant and bored with being alone. Tommy was easy to like; hairdressers, through long experience, can talk endlessly about the trivia of life. I was able to sit back and listen, trying to close my mind to the events of the past few days. It made the beginning of my new life more bearable. Of course I was filled with anxieties. Leaving a husband is rarely an easy thing to do. When I forgot to listen to Tommy's chatter and let my mind wander, I was immediately beset by worries. Could I earn enough to keep Brian and myself? I'd been told that all I could legally expect from Burt for Brian's upkeep was sixteen shillings a week (eighty pence). And as I had deserted Burt he need not pay me a penny. Not that I wanted money from Burt. Somehow I must find a way to support my son and myself.

The other usherettes at the Leicester Square Empire where I was now working were full of advice. 'If you need extra money,' said my friend Doris, 'why don't you work evenings in the theatre?'

'All right. What must I do?'

'Become a dresser. Most of the theatres get short of dressers. I've worked at the London Hippodrome myself looking after the chorus. They pay you fifteen shillings a show and if you work hard you can earn up to six pounds a week.'

Being an usherette in a cinema didn't take any particular skill, but dressing the chorus, that was something else. I kept asking questions.

'The main thing,' said Doris, 'is to be very quick and tidy and have a good memory. You'll soon get the hang of it.'

The next evening when I was on early shift at the Empire I went along to the stage door of the London Hippodrome and asked to speak to the manager. Just as Doris had rehearsed me, I said, 'Any dressing jobs going this evening. Are you a dresser short?'

The manager gave me a cursory glance, 'Any experience?'

'Oh yes,' I said eagerly, 'plenty.'

'Union card?'

'Of course,' I'd had my first union card years ago when Peggy and I had been film extras at Shepherd's Bush Studios.

'Okay,' said the manager, 'report to the wardrobe mistress.'

The wardrobe mistress said, 'It's all downstairs lined up on the racks, you know what to do, don't you? Hunting scene first. Don't forget to bring me all the washing at the end of the last show.'

Everybody assumed that I must know what to do, and it couldn't be all that difficult if they just let you loose on ten defenceless chorus girls. Backstage wasn't the disappointment it might have been for I'd seen the mess and muddle of a film studio and I was used to stepping over cables and minding my head. Bleak distempered brick walls a long rectangle of a dressing room and racks of costumes in the corridor. 'Hunting scene, first,' the wardrobe mistress had said, so the blouses, leather jerkins and short pants must be the first rack. It wasn't too hard, every change was lined up neatly on the racks, shoes underneath, hats on top.

I wasn't too keen on all these rows of hooks and eyes to be done up. Doris explained that zip fasteners were never used for fear of sticking or breaking during a rapid change. 'And don't sew them into their costumes whatever you do, its bad luck.'

'What if something splits?'

'If you do have to sew, make sure you stick the needle into them when you finish.'

'Thanks,' I said, imagining what an irate chorus girl could say.

'They don't mind. They understand, it's to

keep bad luck away.'

What I had forgotten was that chorus girls are kind and human, and they went out of their way to be helpful when they discovered this was my first job. 'Your hands were trembling so much I knew you were a greenhorn,' said one pretty blonde. 'Here, Judy, do me up at the back, give Rose a breather.'

'Don't worry, Rose,' said Judy, 'we'll look after you. Just pick up after us and make sure there's not too much bum showing. These shorts are downright disgusting.'

They were already trouping into the wings when I heard the first surge of music as the orchestra swung into the overture, the rolls of drums, the clash of cymbals. Nothing was ever so exciting to me as that loud, brassy kind of music that opened a Variety show. For a moment I felt let down that I was left here waiting in the wings while the radiant young girls of the chorus, long limbs flashing, went into their opening number. This was always happening to me, always the helper never the performer. The entertainer who never entertained. Then I remembered the girls would be off in five minutes and I had to change them. I hurried back to my next rack of costumes.

At the end of the second show the girls showed me how to bundle together all the used underwear, the tights, the frilly panties and the bras and take them up to the wardrobe mistress, so that they could be washed and made ready for tomorrow's performance.

I sat on the tube train to Harrow very pleased with the thirty shillings I'd earned and ready to go back for another go tomorrow. It became a regular thing for me to work as a dresser in the evening either at the Hippodrome, the Prince of Wales, or Her Majestys', and on a very good week I could make as much as six pounds. Even today a girl can still go round to the stage door of any theatre and ask 'Are you a dresser short?' And she'd probably earn a great deal more than fifteen shillings a show.

★   ★   ★

It was taking me much longer than I'd imagined to adjust to being a woman on her own. I think the fear of loneliness must often send married couples who have separated back together. I was lonely, I was worried, but in my heart I knew I should not go back to Burt. I couldn't take that kind of existence anymore and I thought that Brian was happier than he'd been for months.

As soon as I left Burt, I wrote my mother and father a long letter trying to explain what had happened without painting too black a picture of my life with Burt. When I knew they'd had the letter, posts were very prompt and reliable in those days, I went out to Acton to see them. I sensed the strained atmosphere as soon as I walked in. My father's first words were, 'We think you're making a mistake, Rose. Marriages aren't meant to be broken. We know that Burt has his faults, but he wants you back. He's left a letter for you to read. He wants you to meet him. For our sake, will you do this before you make a final decision?'

Burt's letter when I read it was one long heart-throb. His life was empty without me. He hadn't slept, he couldn't eat. No matter how unkind he'd been, if I would return our life together would be different. I must meet him to talk. And if I didn't want to come back to him, we must meet to discuss Brian's future.

I told my parents that I was living with Tommy in Harrow and how Brian could go to school there and how Tommy would look after him until I returned from work.

My father wouldn't consider such a suggestion. 'Brian is going to stay with us. He's at home here, he's settled. If the worst comes to the worst he can go back to his old school. We must protect the boy whatever happens.' He looked at me severely as if I was trying to shelve my responsibilities.

For the first time since I'd left Burt I wanted to cry. Couldn't my father understand that one of the reasons I'd walked out of my marriage was because of Brian. Keeping a marriage

together because of the child, didn't work. I
was trying to support my son, I wanted to plan
my new life around him. I learnt a lesson that
day. You can plan your own life but it's hard to
make the right decisions for others. My father
was right. Brian was better off with his
grandparents for the time being. Much as I
wanted him to be with me, it was unfair to
uproot him again.

I met Burt a few days later. We sat in a
tea-shop in Regent Street, where I poured out
tea, ate a fancy cake and listened to Burt. The
theme of his entire conversation was himself
and what was going to happen to him if I wasn't
around to look after him. 'I haven't had a
decent meal since you left. What about my
washing, Rose? I need clean shirts.' His
handsome face was aggrieved. 'You're my wife,
you've got responsibilities. You've always
looked after me. What's going to happen to me.
I can't go home and live with my mother even if
I wanted to.'

'You've always liked her cooking better than
mine,' I said thoughtfully.

'If it's the . . .' he changed his mind and
didn't say 'other women', 'if it's my nights out,
you don't have to worry, you know I'll always
come back to you, Rose.'

'Thanks!' Burt was a young man, he'd get
through quite a number of 'colleagues' before
he finally came home to rest. Funny, I thought

to myself, I've stood the gambling, the privations, the selling up of my dearest possessions, but the one thing I won't stand is another woman. I wasn't going to sit at home and play the long-suffering wife. I'd too much respect for myself as a person. 'Shall we talk about Brian,' I suggested. 'That's why I came here.'

'Oh he's all right,' Burt said impatiently, 'He's being well looked after by your Mum and Dad. It's me, I'm talking about. You can't walk out of our marriage, like this. You're my wife.'

I could, I decided, and this last meeting proved it to me. I felt no resentment, no jealousy, not even pity. I felt nothing. 'I want you to divorce me, Burt,' I said. 'I don't want to get married again but I don't want to live with you anymore.' I couldn't explain to him the multitude of reasons, the fact that I thought there must be more to life than a bad marriage, that it just wasn't enough for me. Maybe I should regret leaving him, but that was my lookout.

The next time I saw my parents we talked for two hours and on this occasion I hid nothing from them. My father patted my shoulder, 'Pick up your life, Rose,' he told me. 'Start again. Your mother and I are behind you.'

*   *   *

I worried that Brian didn't ask me questions. He had settled down in his old school and seemed happy, but he didn't say anything about his father or ask why we were living apart. I visited him without fail every day but he didn't talk much. Once more children were being evacuated from London because of the flying bombs and the rockets and if Brian was sent away he might feel more unsettled than ever.

With ordinary bombing we had known where we were to a certain extent, but with flying bombs and rockets it was impossible to be certain of anything. The sirens would wail, there'd be a ghastly explosion and the dead would lie in the streets. A rocket could ravage a whole street, demolish a block of apartments. A shattering, unexpected explosion was ear-splitting and when a flying bomb cut out overhead the look of panic on people's faces was disturbing.

I didn't care for myself. Since my marriage had broken up I'd developed a strange feeling of anaesthesia. If I looked up and saw the smoke from a giant rocket zooming straight overhead, I'd think, 'So what? If my number's on it, too bad.'

On my way to the tube one morning a rocket exploded and devastated a graveyard in Harrow. I looked at the smoking ruins of the monuments and the upturned coffins. 'They can't be hurt anymore,' I said to myself.

'Maybe they're lucky.'

But Brian was young, he had his life to live and I wanted him to be alive when peace came. A very nice couple in Nottingham took him in. Nottingham in the Midlands was far enough away from the rocket launching sites in Northern France to be a safe area. I went up to see him twice and I remember that on the third time I visited him, we went into the town for our special meal, plaice and chips and wartime fancy cakes that tasted like cement. Brian said in a deliberately nonchalant way, 'How far is London from here, Mum?'

I tried to work it out. 'About one hundred and twenty miles.'

'How long would it take to walk that?'

I now understood the question. 'Too long,' I said. 'You'd never make it.'

When I had a moment alone with her I asked the lady who had taken Brian in, what she thought. 'He's homesick,' she said. 'We love having him, and we do our best, but he misses you. I'll let you know if he doesn't get over it.'

A week later I had a letter from her. She'd seen a sheet hanging out of Brian's bedroom window and found Brian busy tying the other end of it to his bedstead. I wrote and asked if she'd be kind enough to put him on the train and I'd meet him.

My mother and I waited for him at Paddington Station. Coming towards us was this small figure in a long tweed coat and big flat tweed cap holding the guard's hand. My mother caught my arm.

'Oh Rose,' she laughed, 'doesn't he look exactly like Harry Tate?'

My son allowed me to kiss him. 'I've come home,' he said gruffly.

'Good job too,' I said, 'I hoped you would.'

Brian's face lit up into a smile. For the first time for ages I felt reassured about him. He still wasn't saying much, but he wanted to come home to me.

★   ★   ★

Maureen, my Irish girlfriend from Southall, had Canada on the brain. Charlie wanted to emigrate there after the war and she talked of nothing else. Tommy and I used to look at each other and recite parrot fashion together, 'Vancouver's warmer than Toronto, but it's thousands of miles away. Now if we go to Montreal . . .'

'Stop taking the mickey,' admonished Maureen. 'You'll be sorry all right when I've packed up and gone.'

I knew I'd be sorry. Maureen was a wonderful friend. Without her and Tommy I'd never have got through those first few weeks. Women can be a great support to each other in times of trouble, and I thanked a kind providence for these two marvellous friends.

Tommy's pregnancy was almost over. Her baby was due any day and I'd promised to be with her when the time came. Corporal Archie Black, her husband, was stationed up in Yorkshire. I'd met him a couple of times when he came home on leave. He was a dark haired, taciturn man who used to give me a curt good morning then bury his head in a newspaper. I kept out of his way as much as I could. Some men act strange when their wives are pregnant and I'd decided that he was one of those. And perhaps being a hairdresser by trade had soured him against women.

Tommy's pains began early one Sunday morning. I went with her in the taxi and waited all day at the hospital until her baby boy was born. When it was all over I went in to see her. Her pretty childish face looked tired but she was very happy. 'Would you let Archie know?' she asked me. 'He said they'd give him compassionate leave when the baby came.'

When I got home I telephoned his camp in Yorkshire and asked to speak to his Commanding Officer. They put me on to the adjutant. 'Corporal Black's wife has just had her baby,' I told him. 'She hopes that her husband will be granted compassionate leave.'

There was quite a pause at the other end. 'When did the baby arrive?' the adjutant questioned.

'A couple of hours ago,' I said brightly. 'It's a little boy, won't he be pleased.'

There was another strange pause. 'Who's that speaking?' asked the officer.

'I'm Mrs Neighbour, I live with Mrs Black.'

'I see,' the adjutant cleared his throat. 'Corporal Black seems to have had second sight for he asked for compassionate leave last Thursday. You're quite sure the baby wasn't born last Thursday?'

This time I paused to think things over. Eventually I said, 'Something's gone wrong somewhere. We'll just have to wait, I suppose until Corporal Black turns up.'

The adjutant made a last effort to salvage the situation. "Sorry to leave you holding the baby and that kind of thing. Of course, he might have missed his connection.'

So Archie had been on compassionate leave for the past four days and he hadn't made it down to Harrow yet. Even if he'd missed every connection from Crewe to London he should have got here by now.

I couldn't tell Tommy, but I needed some advice so I telephoned Tommy's mother in Westgate. She was overjoyed about the baby and seemed to take the news of Archie's disappearance stoically. Straight away she launched into a blistering attack on her son-in-law. 'I never liked him from the first time I saw him. Have you noticed that shifty look in his eyes. I always knew he wasn't good enough for my daughter. He's with some other woman, that's where he is, the dirty, rotten, no good . . .' the acid fairly flowed and I thought whatever happens, poor old Tommy is going to get a rough deal.

It turned out to be true. Archie had gone away for a long weekend with a Yorkshire lass. Having a last fling before settling down to the trials of fatherhood, perhaps. But Tommy did not look at it that way. 'There was I in agony,' she told me, sitting up in bed at the hospital, looking like a sexy choir boy, 'lying on my bed of pain having his baby while he was in a double bed with this Yorkshire bird. She can keep him, I don't want him. He was always a rotten hairdresser. Did I tell you about the time he turned some woman's hair green?'

Fortunately, Tommy was a good hairdresser and had money in the bank. Most of the furniture in the Harrow house belonged to her and she even paid the rent. 'Archie's had it,' she said. 'We're finished. As long as I'm in this house he'll never set foot in it again.'

It did me good to hear a woman talking who could take care of herself and her newborn son. But when I had time to think about it I was astounded at the way marriages were breaking up all around. Mine and Tommy's, and even Maureen's had come close to a break-up too. I blamed the war, taking men away from their

wives, bringing women into the army, the fields
and the factories. Later I thought it might have
been the birth of a new kind of woman who
would rather go it alone than be kicked around
by men. Whatever it was, I'd joined their
ranks.

*　　　*　　　*

London in the winter of 1944 was filled with
American servicemen. This generated a certain
amount of jealousy from the native born sons,
for the American boys looked so smart in their
olive green compared to the British rough khaki
uniforms. But the local girls had a ball. The
Americans not only had the appeal of being
from far off places and full of surprises, but
they were well paid, generous and gave the girls
a good time. All around the West End there
were groups of young Americans eyeing the
dames and the air around Piccadilly
reverberated with wolf whistles.

It was the easiest thing in the world to let an
American soldier pick you up, but I wasn't
having any. I was off men, English, Polish,
Canadian or American. Every day I showed
servicemen of all nationalities to their seats at
the Leicester Square Empire and I was able to
resist their invitations quite easily.

On this particular afternoon trade in the
cinema was slack before the rush started when

the shops closed. I was having a few minutes rest watching the ladylike acting of Irene Dunne when an American serviceman came through the curtains behind me. He stood hesitantly, then held a ticket out to me.

I examined it under my torch light. 'You're in the wrong place,' I said, 'you want the circle upstairs.'

'It doesn't matter,' he had one of those five fathoms underwater American voices, 'I'll be happy to stay here.'

'Oh no, it's more expensive in the circle and you've paid the money. Just follow me.' I led him back through the swing doors to the brightly lit foyer, 'Over there,' I pointed to the stairs, 'you can't miss it.'

'I'd just as soon stay down here with you.'

I smiled. Here we go again, I thought. 'You'll see much better up there.' Then I turned and went back to the stalls before the young soldier could think up the next line of the routine chatting up.

When I left the cinema at about eight that evening on my way to the Leicester Square underground station to take my tube home, a man came up to me. At first it took me a moment to recognise him, but the high lace up boots and the white Penguin insignia on the sleeve of his American uniform jogged my memory. It was the soldier I'd sent up to the circle. He must have waited out here for a long time.

He saluted, 'Pardon me, Ma'am . . .' the American boys were always so polite. 'I was wondering . . . ?'

'Sorry,' I'd learned that the quick brush off was best. 'I'm on my way home.'

'Could I walk you home?' he asked eagerly.

'It'll be a long walk. I live in Harrow.'

'Harrow? Where's that?'

I studied him for a moment. He was tall and well built, about five foot eleven, and under his service cap his hair showed dark. He was lonely, of course, they were all lonely. 'There are lots of places for servicemen around here, you know.' I suggested, 'There's the American Rainbow Club on the corner.'

His smile was diffident. 'When you're stationed on a base full of guys, you don't want to spend your furlough with them.'

'Well there's the Regent Palace Hotel.'

'Where's that ma'am?'

'Straight along Piccadilly. You can't miss it?'

His smile grew broader. 'That's the second time you've said that, "you can't miss it", let me tell you ma'am I'm a stranger here. Would you care to have a drink with me there?'

'I don't drink?'

'Maybe a soda?'

'Soda water?' Then I realised he meant a soft drink. I also realised that I was standing in front of the cinema talking to a strange man, an

American at that, and I was enjoying it. He had a nice open boyish face. Why shouldn't I go mad and have a drink with him? 'I won't be able to stay long,' I insisted, and then I added, in an attempt to damp down any ideas he might have, 'I promised I'd call in and see my son.'

'Your son? Are you married? You sure don't look old enough.' It was nice to listen to such flattery from a man, nice to forget for a moment that I was thirty-three years old and I'd finished with the fun and games of being young.

'No, I'm not married anymore.' I walked with him towards Piccadilly and the Regent Palace Hotel catching sight of our reflection in a shop window, a small woman in a worn tweed coat that I'd bought before the war and this tall young American.

His name was Carl Zapczi, he told me, I had trouble trying to pronounce it, and he was from West Virginia. 'Ever heard of West Virginia, ma'am?' he asked me as we sat down at a table in the side lobby of the hotel.

'Of course I have,' I said sharply, 'they do educate us over here. And stop calling me ma'am. You make me feel like a schoolteacher. My name's Rose.'

Now that I could see him clearly, I realised that he had a foreign look, not American as I imagine Americans should look, darker more Spanish looking or Jewish. He saw me staring at him. 'My family came from Rumania,' he

145

said. 'I'm second generation.'

'Go on! How'd they get to West Virginia?'

'Well you see there was this old guy. He had three mines and he had three daughters, so he called each mine after one of his daughters. When my Dad arrived at Ellis Island, and said he was a coal miner, they said, "Which mine d'you want to go to, Anna Maria, Louisa or Caroline?" and my Dad picked Anna Maria because he'd once had a girlfriend with that name.' There was a twinkle in his eye as he watched my face.

'Go on,' I said, 'you're pulling me leg.'

'Honest to God, I'm not. I grew up in a mining village in West Virginia.'

'Good Lord, you're a coal miner too?'

Carl laughed, 'Not me. After I quit school I went up to Detroit and got me a job with Ford.'

Later, he walked me to the underground station outside the hotel then he asked me if I'd meet him next day, Saturday, and have dinner with him. 'No strings,' he said, 'just the pleasure of your company . . . Rose.'

'Okay,' I started to go down the steps, 'four thirty under the clock at Victoria Station.'

He started after me, 'Where's the clock?'

I laughed, 'You can't miss it.'

*   *   *

It was cold and windy next day. I put a scarf

over my hair as I came up the underground steps. I wasn't at all sure that he'd be there. I wasn't even sure if I wanted him to be. The quick drink after work last night had been really nice, but now in the daylight it might be another story. Maybe I wouldn't even recognise him.

He shouted when he saw me, 'Hi, honey!' and lifted his hand in welcome. He was there, looking bandbox smart, fresh and clean and young. After experiencing four long years of bombing, rockets, lack of sleep and ration books, to me he looked so healthy that it didn't seem fair.

'I found it,' he called. 'I found the clock.' There it was way above his head, the big clock at the entrance to Victoria Station, the meeting place of a hundred, thousand Londoners. He took my arm, as if he'd known me for years. 'Take a look,' he said, 'I feel I'm really in London, England.' The big red buses rattled by, the crowds hurried into the station, the pigeons strutted in search of crumbs and from inside the station came the ear-splitting noises as the trains came in and blew off steam against the high glass roof.

We had dinner at Maxim's in Leicester Square, because it was one of the few places I had ever been to before. I told him about Henry the optician who had brought me here years ago. We laughed together when I told him of the scandalous finale when Henry put his hand up my skirt.

'Playing hard to get, eh?' Carl said with a grin.

'I was impossible to get,' I insisted. 'Girls in those days—didn't. Full stop.'

'You're making yourself sound like an old woman. You're not old.'

'I'm thirty-three. How old are you?'

'Twenty-eight. So that's just dandy.'

I shook my head. 'You're too young. And I don't want any man, young or old.'

'Are you warning me off, honey?'

'Yes.'

'Okay,' he said, 'you're the boss.'

He told me about the small town he came from in West Virginia.

'It's a big country compared to England. Big trees, big fields. Our town's in a valley. There's nothing much there, the post office, the store, the school and of course the Church.'

'Church?' I asked. 'Are you Protestant?'

'No. Catholic. My folks go to mass regular, but I'm not so good.'

'And your house? What kind of a house do you live in?'

'Frame. What you'd call timber. It's raised up because of the winter snows. We get a hot summer, but sometimes real cold winters.'

I sat and listened as we ate the Chinese food, enthralled at the glimpse he was giving me of a new country, a foreign way of life. In the weeks that followed every time we met he told me more about America and I showed him London. He told me he'd never walked so far in his life, but I assured him that it was the only way to understand what London was all about. I showed him the bombed church of St Mary Le Bow in Cheapside, St Paul's in the City. 'Have you ever heard of Bow Bells? Well this is where they ring. If you're born within the sound of Bow Bells then you're a real cockney.'

'Are you a cockney, Rose?'

'No, I was born in West London, and this is East. I'm just a Londoner.'

Carl was stationed in Colchester, Essex. Sometimes he couldn't make it to London when he hoped and he'd send me a telegram. I knew then he was off on one of his missions. He was with a paratroop unit. I didn't really know where he went or what he did. In wartime you didn't ask questions and no soldier passed information on to a civilian.

We didn't kiss. We didn't hold hands. We just liked being together. I told none of my family about my new friend, only Tommy. She asked me to bring him over to Harrow for supper one Sunday. I remember we got into the underground train and Carl lit up one of his Lucky Strikes. I didn't smoke in those days and paid no attention to the fact that we were in a non-smoking compartment. An irate lady soon drew our attention to the non-smoking notice. At the next station we decided to get out. He caught my hand as we ran laughing along the platform to change compartments, held me when I tripped. He was still holding my hand when we sank down breathless into a seat. My ankle hurt and I bent down and took off my shoe. He held my shoe in his hand, it was worn, with a cobbler's stitching holding the side together, and I would rather he hadn't examined it.

Tommy liked him. 'He's a very nice man,' she said.

'He's just a boy.'

'He doesn't look like a boy to me, and he doesn't look at you like a boy would. If I had half a chance I'd snap him up myself.'

'I've a son to bring up, Tommy. Even if I wanted to, I wouldn't have a wartime romance.' Tommy's smile was slightly cynical. 'Watch it,' she said, 'your halo's showing.'

Carl, like most American servicemen was generosity itself. Every time he came to Harrow he brought Hershey chocolate bars for baby Roger who hadn't grown a tooth yet, soap, coffee and tea for Tommy, and for me there was always a lipstick, a pair of nylon stockings or a bottle of scent. Once he bought a parcel for me that his mother had sent. In it were a pair of black suede high-heeled shoes with sling backs. The kind we only saw in American movies and never, ever would find in our war torn shoe shops, even if we had the coupons to spare.

'Try 'em on,' he ordered, 'see if they fit.' They did perfectly.

'How on earth . . . ?' I began.

'Remember when you slipped on the subway?' He grinned at me. 'Mom's written you a letter. Here take it.'

Because of the journey back to London and the fact that she had a spare room, Tommy asked him to stay the night once, and it became a habit. Sometimes when it was time to go to bed, I'd see him looking at me, and I knew Tommy was watching us with a secret smile, but I was determined to keep the relationship as it was. If I'd been honest with myself I would have admitted that I was falling in love with Carl, that the weekends when he came were some of the happiest times I'd had in my life, but I wasn't honest.

One Saturday Tommy had a phone call from her mother in Westgate and she decided she'd better go down and see her. 'Can I trust you on your own with Carl,' she asked with a twinkle in her eye.

I was just going to bed when I remembered I hadn't put any clean towels in his room; Carl liked a bath in the morning. I put on my dressing gown, found the towels and tapped nervously on the door of the spare room. He smiled when he saw me, put down the book he was reading and said, 'Don't stand there. Come on in.'

'It's late,' I said, laying the towels over the edge of his bed. Already I was backing out of the room. 'Goodnight, sleep well.'

'Rose!' his voice was puzzled. 'Why are you so scared?'

'I don't know what you mean.'

'You act like I'm some kind of bad guy.'

That was the last thing he was. A kinder, more sincere man I had never known. 'When my marriage broke up,' I said hesitantly, 'I swore I'd never let another man hurt me.'

'We all get hurt,' he said gently. 'Come and sit down.' He patted the bed at his side. 'Just for a while, let's sit and talk.'

I sat on the edge of the bed, drawing the neckline of my dressing gown prudishly together . . .

'You're trying to push men out of life Rose, and you're all wrong. Men and women need each other. Especially in the bad times, like now!' His hand reached out for mine.

'I'd better go,' I whispered. 'It's late.'

'Sometimes Rose, I don't sleep nights. What's happening next day weighs you down. We're not all heroes, I'm as scared as the next guy. But when the mood comes over me I try and think of you. The way your hair waves over your forehead . . . the way you laugh . . .'

'I'm glad.'

'They shouldn't frighten you these feelings of mine. You can't go through life being scared of men. I like being with you. You like being with me. What's so wrong with that?' I started to get up, but his hand held mine. 'Rose don't you like me at all?'

I looked at him. I liked his dark eyes and the kindness I saw in them. I liked the way he looked, not that he was handsome but he had such a nice face. I smiled. 'You know I like you.'

I knew he was going to kiss me. I wanted him to. I wanted everything that happened that night. And when the morning came and I saw him asleep next to me, I no longer just liked him, I loved him. If he opened his eyes and said to me, 'Rose, stay with me always,' I'd stay. If he said, 'Come with me, wherever I go, you follow,' I'd follow. I'd want to grab Brian by the hand and take him with me, but if Carl asked me to go anywhere with him, I'd go like a shot.

CHAPTER EIGHT

PICKING UP THE PIECES

We leaned over Westminster Bridge. The Thames below us looked grey and oily in the bleak March sunshine. 'Now the river back home,' said Carl, 'goes bright red in the summer. Something to do with the minerals, they say. But when you drive past it a day later, it'll be blue, as blue as your eyes, honey.'

'Washed out old British blue, I know what you mean.' I laughed at him. 'Go on, tell me more about your river. What's it like?' Our sightseeing walks around London were usually accompanied by Carl's comparisons with his home town in West Virginia. I loved to hear him talk. I couldn't hear enough about America, about the mine at Anna Maria, even about giant, dirty Pittsburgh, the big city.

Carl put his arm through mine as we walked along. 'You'll get off the plane at Pittsburgh,' he said, 'and I'll be waiting for you. I'll be driving a new Ford convertible, or if it hasn't been delivered by the time you arrive, I'll have Dad's old Studebaker. Takes about two and half hours to drive home.'

'And if I can't get a seat on a plane? If I have to come by sea?'

'Okay, honey, I'll be right there in New York waiting for you.'

'D'you think your family will like me?'

'Honey, my folks will be crazy about you. And boy, won't they be tickled pink. My Dad said "now don't go falling for any of those English girls" and what did I say, "not on your life Dad!" And then what does this clean cut

154

young American do. He takes one look at a certain English gal, and zowie . . .'

I knew it was a game we were playing. How could I go to America? I wasn't even divorced from Burt. But somehow, someday, I prayed that this game would become reality. Sometimes I looked at Carl, my heart brimming over with love, and I thought to myself, 'It's too good to be true, Rose. Take hold of yourself, stop dreaming. Life can't be this good.'

It was March 1945 and the war had to be over soon. That was all we needed. Never in my life had I been so happy; it was as if the band of tension and worry I'd felt around my head since my marriage had collapsed, had been severed. My love for Carl was very different from the way I had loved Burt. That had been the love of a young, inexperienced girl which had slowly been eroded by the disappointments of our life together. This time my love was different, I was older and I didn't expect too much. Every day of happiness was a gift and I was thankful.

For the first time in my life I had a man I could not only love but talk to. How we talked, about every blessed thing. 'I'll be happy when you leave the Empire,' Carl told me, 'it's not the right work for you, Rose. Your work should bring you happiness.' He had a philosophy about life that was new to me. He was a thoughtful man, and in me he had found the perfect listener.

Only my sister Grace and Tommy knew about my love affair with Carl. My parents had been upset by the break-up of my marriage and I couldn't give them fresh worries, but as soon as my divorce from Burt was on the way I would be free to tell them. As for my son Brian, I needed time to break the news to him slowly. I felt sure he would like Carl—the ties with his father were slackening for Burt rarely bothered to visit him, even so, I couldn't risk Brian being hurt. Let well alone, I decided.

It was enough to have these weekends of sheer happiness. Days like today when we'd met as usual under the clock at Victoria. We still had an hour or two before it was dark to walk around and delight in just being together.

'What shall we do later?' Carl asked. 'How about a night out on the town. Shall we go dancing, taking in some wild night club?'

'I don't want to sit in a smoky old night club. Why don't we buy some fruit and sit and eat it in the park. Then we'll go back to Harrow and I'll cook you a meal.' I gave him a sidelong look, 'Tommy's away tonight. She's gone to her mother at Westgate.'

Carl grinned at me. 'I offer the lady a night out on the town and what does she want. A walk in the park and a ride on the subway!'

I knew he was joking. Carl was a home lover. He was always happy pottering about Tommy's house, doing the odd jobs that needed attention, 'tending the furnace and mending the faucets', as he said. I believed Carl when he told me that he wanted to settle down, get married, have children and live with me forever.

That night we talked, how we talked. It was five o'clock before we slept.

On Sunday morning we were up early for Carl had to get back to base by noon. He'd had his bath, dressed and was downstairs sitting in a chair lacing up his high boots.

I knelt at his feet, 'I'll do this for you,' I said.

'Don't you dare,' he said in a shocked voice. 'Don't you ever dare do that.'

'Why not?'

'No woman has to kneel at my feet and lace my boots.'

I smiled up at him, 'Carl I want to lace your boots. I want you to go back to base wearing boots I've laced, because I love you and this is my way of showing it.'

As I worked on the tough laces his hand touched my hair. He didn't stroke it, he just patted it gently. When I'd finished he drew me to my feet, he said softly. 'There'll never be anyone but you for me, Rose. I promise.'

*   *   *

Carl was late that next Saturday. In all the months, ever since I'd known him, for the first time, Carl was late. Had he sent me a telegram

157

to say he wasn't coming, I wondered. Surely not, or else Tommy would have telephoned me at the Empire to let me know.

So I worried. I walked back and forth under the archway of the station, down the arcade, back again. I walked and I worried. When I'd been waiting for over an hour I was almost distraught. Something has happened, I told myself. Please God, don't let it be true. But something must have happened.

I noticed a young American serviceman staring at me. I'd seen him before watching me. Our eyes met for an instant. I saw him hesitate, start forwards towards me, then hesitate again. At last he seemed to pluck up enough nerve to speak to me.

'Pardon me, ma'am.'

'What d'you want?' I said abruptly. I was in no mood to chat about the quickest way to Buckingham Palace.

The young man faltered, but he tried again. 'I beg your pardon, ma'am, if I'm wrong, but are you by chance waiting for someone?'

'Of course I am.'

'Is it . . .' he gulped 'Carl?'

I stared at him. 'How do you know?'

'Then your name's Rose, isn't it, ma'am?' Something told me that whatever message this young man was going to give me it wouldn't be welcome. He had a fresh young face with rosy cheeks but I could see beads of perspiration on his forehead.

'Is anything the matter?'

He moistened his lips. 'Ma'am, Miss Rose . . .' his voice was different to Carl's, slow and drawling, from the Deep South, 'I've got bad news for you. Carl didn't make it back last night. He was on a mission over Germany.'

I opened my mouth to ask what he meant but no words came out. The young man's face became pale, I literally saw the colour leave his face. 'The plane was lost. No news of survivors.'

On the other side of Victoria a red double-decker bus drew up. I turned and stared at it, watched it fade away, then come back into focus again, as if someone was squeezing my eyes. The stone pavings under my feet began to quiver, they felt soft as if I was sinking through them. From far away I heard the young soldier's voice, 'Are you all right, Miss Rose?' I realised that his arm was around me and that I was swaying. Gradually the earth beneath my feet stopped moving. The red bus became an ordinary bus again, and the face of the young serviceman looked down at me. He looked so stricken and white that I wanted to comfort him. My voice came back. I thanked him for coming. Yes, I was all right. Just the shock. But I was all right now.

'I'm so sorry, ma'am. Carl was a real good guy. He'd have wanted me to come and find you. "Under the clock at Victoria", that's what he used to say. I've been back so many times today, Miss Rose.'

'It's so good of you. So kind. Thank you. No, don't stay. I'd rather go home.' I started to walk away. I didn't know why. I didn't know where I was until I saw the wooden benches inside the station. I clung to the edge as I sat down, my legs felt strange and my head hurt with the noise around me. Steam hissed from the stationary engines, a whistle echoed off the glass roof, and the sound of people's voices grew into a thunderous roar. There were so many people, people in khaki, air force blue, and as they rushed past me they seemed to dissolve into a mist. I don't know how long I sat there. The noise rose and fell, it came, it went. At one time I looked up and saw the young American serviceman in front of me again. He held out his hand as if saying goodbye. I took it and we shook hands formally. I thanked him again.

I saw him walk away. He was such a polite young man, I thought, just like Carl . . . and then, I remembered and I was sane again. Carl was dead. He wouldn't wait for me under the clock at Victoria ever again. He wouldn't eat hard English pears in Hyde Park and tell me, 'Honey, we sure grow better pears than this back home.' Carl was a splendid man and he was dead. What a waste. What a terrible waste. He'd be just another name on a war memorial, but to me he was so much more. He was my love and he had loved me.

I began to tremble with emotion. Tears pricked my eyes. I shook my head angrily. I wouldn't cry. Too many tears were being shed in this rotten war. I got up and walked down to the underground and the lump in my throat grew so big that I thought I would choke.

*   *   *

Not long ago, in this year of 1978, I watched a television film, one of the Kojak series with Telly Savalas. An old song was played in it called, 'For all we know'. It was a great favourite about the time I knew Carl. It wasn't our song, but we both liked it. I listened to the words of the lyric again '. . . for all we know, we may never meet again . . .' and it all came back to me.

I saw Carl's face again. I heard his lovely deep timbred American voice calling out, 'Hi, honey!' and I remembered the way I'd felt about him. There'd been so little time for us, but every day, each time we met, had been like a celebration. How I'd loved him. If he'd said, 'Pack your bags, Rose, we're leaving.' I'd have gone with him at once, without question.

The words and music blared from the television and I began to cry. I cried as if my heart was breaking. All over again.

Looking back I know that Carl's death was an emotionally shattering blow for me. For the first time in my life I had loved someone to the exclusion of all else. And yet his death helped me to discover myself. With him every hour, every day had been savoured and I realised that was the way I should live. Banal as it sounds, Carl had made me a woman again, he had taught me that living meant loving, not feeling bitterness and distrust.

I changed my job after Carl died. Ever since my marriage broke up I'd been working flat out, determined to make as much money as I could, even doing a second job in the theatre in the evenings. Money wasn't all that important I decided. Brian was well looked after, well fed, and all I was doing was trying to prove to myself that I could earn a living as well as any man.

I'd found out that I could and now I wanted to do a job I liked that would give me time to see more of my family. And I wanted to get away from the West End when every time I saw the back of a tall young American soldier I'd have this wild surge of unreasoning hope that it might be Carl. I found a job in Harrow working in a British Restaurant.

'Rose,' said my friend Doris at the Empire cinema when I told her what I was doing. 'You'll hate it. It's all very well saying this is going to be your war effort, but the war's nearly over and these British Restaurants are crummy places like soup kitchens.'

Doris had got it all wrong. To begin with, the British Restaurant in Harrow was one of the best of its kind. After all, the famous school on the hill had once had Winston Churchill as a pupil. And when I found out more about British Restaurants I was quite proud to be one of their staff.

After the terrible bombings in the winter of 1940, homeless and frightened people needed food and shelter, so emergency feeding centres were opened. The Ministry of Food offered each local council throughout the country a government grant so they could start restaurants where every man, woman and child could, if necessary, obtain at least one hot nourishing meal a day at a price they could afford.

Financially, perhaps, I wasn't so well off, but I could walk to my job and my hours were from eight in the morning until five. It was a healthier existence away from the strange twilight world of the cinema and the theatre. And I was with people, listening to their problems and their joys as I served food across the counter.

Carl had also given me a great new interest. America! Every time I read or heard anything about the United States it was as if Carl was there at my side saying, 'Honey, let's rest awhile on that bench and I'll answer your questions one by one. What did you ask? Does every American woman have a washing machine? Well the answer to that is, No.'

Because of Carl I wrote a letter to a journalist called Rose Buckner. She had a column in the *Sunday People* and ran The International Mother's Club. Rose Buckner wanted English children to correspond with American children to increase international friendship. One of her contacts was an American headmaster called Paul Warner, and a pupil of his at the Junior High School in Greenville, Ohio got in touch with Brian and they began corresponding. In time I too, began to write to Paul Warner and his wife Edna and it was the beginning of an important friendship.

Carl had given me a glimpse of the American way of life that I felt instinctively I should love. I realised that America wasn't a classless society, but its barriers must be less rigid and cruel than those in England. I had once overheard a conversation between two women leaving the cinema. They were discussing an acquaintance and one of them said, 'Yes, she's quite a nice woman but I wouldn't invite her to my home. You see she isn't socially acceptable.'

I'd wondered to myself just what 'socially acceptable' meant. I could guess. And I was angry at such snobbery. No woman likes to be put in an inferior compartment by others because her accent isn't the right one or her education had finished at the age of fourteen. Carl had the right idea, I decided, when he'd told me that education goes on right through one's life, and it isn't the school you went to it's the books you read and the openness of your mind.

In the British Restaurant where I now worked I enjoyed talking to people from every walk of life. I had joined the catering industry where there are always vacancies because catering is darned hard work, but I liked it. There were three of us behind the counter, Gladys, a pretty girl with long fair hair who had just married a sailor, and Mary, the cook. Together we made up our own rules of hospitality. Any pregnant woman who came in was always given an extra helping of meat and any child who wanted it always had an extra dollop of pudding. There was no commercial enterprise urging us to cut corners or eke out the rations. We didn't dispense charity, but we were there to keep the nation healthy and help with the war. At least that was our story.

In 1945 a typical lunch we served was roast beef and two vegetables, treacle pudding, bread and butter and a cup of tea or coffee, all for the price of one shilling (five pence).

I remember a pregnant girl who used to come in to eat lunch every day. Her house had been wrecked by a flying bomb and her husband was in Germany. 'I've got this terrible craving for fruit,' she told me. 'I dream every night about peaches. I don't even know what they taste like. I was a kid when the war started but even as a little girl I used to long for a peach when I saw barrow loads of them in Berwick Market.'

I said to Mary, the cook, 'You couldn't get a tin of peaches for her could you?'

'Not a hope,' she said, but every day on our way to work, the three of us used to look in greengrocer's windows just in case there might be a peach for sale. Fruit was hard to come by. One morning Gladys came in holding something wrapped in a piece of tissue paper: it was a ripe, beautiful peach.

'Seven and six,' said Gladys, 'that's half a crown each, please.'

From behind the counter we all watched surreptitiously as the pregnant girl ate it slowly. Her face was expressionless.

'Maybe it's sour,' whispered Gladys.

I couldn't stand it any longer I went out from behind the counter. 'Any good?' I asked airily. She had no idea of the trouble we'd all taken to find it for her.

Suddenly she gave me a radiant smile. 'I don't know how much it cost,' she said, 'but it was worth every penny. Now I know what peaches taste like—like manna from heaven.'

When I came back and reported the success of our operation, Mary the cook said, 'I'm not complaining Rose, but the next pregnant girl you take on had better crave something cheap, like a lump of nice coal.'

Gladys, being a newlywed, never stopped talking about her wonderful husband in the Navy. She used to bring in his letters with her and read them over and over again. He was on a mine-sweeper stationed somewhere off the coast of Scotland, and they wrote to each other every day. The way Gladys wore her hair fascinated me. She'd wind a thick piece of rag around her head, knot it in the centre, then sweep her long mane up into it making a thick roll. She looked splendid, like a film star I used to tell her.

One morning, however, she came in carrying her usual letter and I noticed that her pretty face was downcast. 'I'm terribly worried,' she said, 'Sambo, the ship's cat fell overboard.'

'Never you mind,' laughed Mary, the cook. 'Cats have got nine lives and I bet he's not drowned. Probably sitting on some iceberg.'

'It's not the cat that worries me. It's the bad luck. Perhaps the ship will sink.'

'Oh stop it,' Mary admonished her. 'The war's over. Nobody's going to sink your hubby's ship.'

Although I didn't say anything, I felt just like Gladys. Sambo was a black cat, and I'd always worried about them, never quite sure that if one crossed your path it was good luck or not.

A few weeks later Gladys had a telegram. Her

167

husband had been killed in an explosion aboard his ship.

Although she came back to the restaurant after the funeral her heart wasn't in it any more. I often wonder what happened to her. We gave each other little keepsakes when she left. She gave me a cigarette case with the words 'People who smoke are cheerful folk' stencilled on the front. That wouldn't go down well with the anti-smoking brigade nowadays. But even then when smoking wasn't frowned upon, I sighed as I looked at it. 'You've really gone to the devil, Rose,' I told myself. 'Before your marriage broke up you didn't smoke and you didn't drink. Now you do both.'

★   ★   ★

Victory over Japan, VJ Day, brought tremendous relief to everyone. Happiness touched with sadness for the ones who would never come home again: my cousin Edna's husband who had died defusing a bomb; the young husband of Gladys, and my American, Carl amongst them. Sadness too, as people began to leave England for better opportunities abroad. Maureen and Charlie were off to Canada as soon as they could find a ship. Even Tommy decided to move down to Westgate and live with her mother.

'If Archie thinks I'm going to leave him

anything, he's got another think coming,' declared Tommy. 'He's welcome to move in and pay the rent, but all he'll get is a cup and saucer, a plate and a knife and fork.' Tommy was in the process of divorcing Archie. When she learnt that I was looking for somewhere to live, Grace, my sister, asked me to move in with her at Acton. Grace and I had always been very close, I got on very well with Ronnie her husband and although they had two children. Marianne and Peter, there was a spare bedroom for me. Living at Acton also meant that I should be nearer my parents and my son Brian.

It was in 1947 that I saw this advertisement in the *Evening News* 'Catering Staff wanted for the BBC'. British Restaurants were closing down and it was only a matter of time before the one in Harrow followed suit.

I talked it over with Grace. 'Be nice if I could work in the Light Programme with Tommy Handley and people like that,' I told her. The Light Programme encompassed all manner of variety and musical shows and it had taken over from the General Forces Programme after the war.

The British Broadcasting Company had a very special place in the hearts of everyone who'd lived through the war in Britain. At the touch of a switch, comfort and entertainment were always there. We accepted every BBC news bulletin as the word of truth and the

Company well deserved the fine reputation it had built up. I remembered way back when the BBC came into existence in 1922, and how slowly it took on the role of giving public service. Like everyone else I'd grown up listening to the wireless.

I dressed with particular care for the interview. Because we were still on clothes coupons it wasn't always easy to follow the fashions and we hadn't a hope of copying Christian Dior's New Look that was sweeping France, so I did what we all did in those days, I borrowed. First a smart costume from Grace, then a hat from a girlfriend and a pair of white gloves from my mother.

Before the war the seven floors of gleaming white stone in Portland Place had been a show place, but Broadcasting House was now grey and battered. It had suffered a direct hit from a time bomb and had been ravaged by fire when a land-mine exploded in Portland Place. Even so it had survived, there was a uniformed commissionaire and the entrance hall was still grand enough to impress me.

The Catering Supervisor had grey hair and was called Miss Thackwray. The first thing she said was, 'Are you married? If you are this job might not be suitable for the hours are long and sometimes uncertain.'

I said I was separated from my husband and I was used to long hours. Miss Thackwray looked relieved, 'I'm so glad for if you're not a clock watcher you'll enjoy working at the Paris.'

'The Paris?' I said anxiously, 'but I've come to work at the BBC.'

'So you will. We took over the Paris cinema in Regent Street for variety shows. I'm sure you've heard of them—Tommy Handley's *ITMA*, for instance?'

She couldn't have said anything to interest me more.

Tommy Handley!

The Paris cinema in Lower Regent Street was about five minutes away from Broadcasting House. As we walked there Miss Thackwray explained that the tea-bar, which I was to run, had lately been a hit and miss affair. 'And it's so unfair on the artistes and musicians not to have proper refreshment. They'll be very pleased to see you.'

The little cinema, down two flights of stairs, had been turned into a studio, although to my eyes it still looked like a real theatre with a wide stage and rows of seats for an invited audience. At the back of the theatre were the glassed in compartments for the production and recording teams. Left of these, behind the stalls was a corridor, through it we came to a closed hatchway. Miss Thackwray flung open a door at the side. 'I'm afraid it's rather untidy,' she said uncertainly.

I looked inside and at once my jaw dropped.

171

It was filthy, and to my first startled glance looked more like a dungeon than a tea-bar.

Miss Thackwray saw my reaction. 'We could move things around and provide more space,' she suggested hopefully.

Throw things out, you mean, I thought to myself. It looked like a disaster area, the rusty door of the fridge hung open, an ancient tea-urn rested near a cracked china sink. On the shelves were rows of old chipped cups and saucers with the grime of years engrained in them. After the spotless kitchen and restaurant in Harrow, the BBC tea-bar was a gruesome sight. All I wanted to do was get out of the Paris cinema as soon as I could and catch the first bus to Acton.

Miss Thackwray tried again. 'We could throw everything out and start again with fresh equipment?'

She was such a nice person that I knew I might weaken unless I made a move. 'I'm sorry,' I began as I edged along the corridor. Outside in the theatre someone touched the keys of a piano. A tinkling cascade of sound followed as the played executed some intricate chords.

Miss Thackwray saw me hesitate. 'Do you like music, Mrs Neighbour?'

'Oh yes, I love music.'

'You'll have so much music down here. The best orchestras, the big bands . . . we could have a new fridge, new kitchen furniture . . .'

her eyes were begging me to stay. 'It would be a challenge, don't you think, Mrs Neighbour, making a little haven for all these artistes?'

All the big names. Tommy Handley, Ben Lyon, Bebe Daniels . . . Oh go on, Rose, I told myself, say yes, and Miss Thackwray's so nice too . . . 'If I'm going to work here,' I said, 'you'd better call me Rose, and the sooner this place is cleaned up the better.'

Miss Thackwray was off at once crying, 'Don't go away, I'll be right back,' and so she was with a porter carrying brooms and buckets and packets of soda and soap powder. I removed the white gloves, the hat and Grace's best suit, wrapped myself in a large green overall the BBC had provided and got to work. That piano player certainly could play. I wondered who he was. Just as long as he kept on I was quite happy cleaning up the filthy kitchen. Then the music stopped. Someone came down the corridor shouting, 'Anybody there? Anybody there?' Shall I answer, I thought and decided that in this large overall with my hair tied up in a duster I looked too much of a sight to see anyone.

A short time later I heard footsteps in the alleyway outside the back door to the kitchen. The same voice called, 'Who's there?' and banged on the wooden panels. This time I did answer. An astonished young man stood outside. 'Who are you?' he asked.

'My name's Rose Neighbour and I'm going to run this tea-bar.'

He beamed. 'My God, that's good news. Any chance of a cuppa?'

'Who are you I might ask?'

'I'm Colin Farnell. I'm Orchestra Manager with the Stanley Black orchestra. The boys in the band will all be here directly. Will you really make us a cup of tea. They won't believe it when I tell them.'

'If you like to find a dairy and buy some bottles of milk and some tea and sugar, I certainly will.'

'Oh thanks, you're a darling. What did you say your name was?'

'Rose! Here d'you want a basket to put the bottles in?'

He was off and I lit the gas under the rusty old kettle. I was back in the free and easy world of entertainment. Somehow I knew that this was it. I'd found the right niche. Just like Carl had always said. The right work can give you so much happiness.

CHAPTER NINE

TEA AND SYMPATHY AT THE BBC

Peter came in through the back door of my kitchen. The entrance from the alley that ran at the back of the Paris cinema. The entrance reserved for my favourites and those in the know. He sat down with a heart rending sigh. 'It's all off, Rose,' he said dejectedly. 'She's thrown me over.' His plump young face that one day would smile from hoardings all over the world, looked miserable enough to dissolve into tears.

I switched on the electric kettle and rinsed out the tea-pot. Peter always liked a strong cup of tea. 'Never mind, love,' I commiserated as I spooned in three measures of tea. 'Maybe she wasn't the right one for you.'

It was Peter's first big love affair. He'd been telling me about it for weeks. She was a nurse and they were going to get married. Because he wasn't the kind of man to play around, the break-up of his romance hit him hard. If anyone had told me that one day Peter Sellers would have the reputation of a lady-killer, I wouldn't have believed them. If anyone had told me that Peter would get through four marriages and hit the headlines with torrid romances with Sophia Loren, Liza Minelli and other ladies I would have said, 'Never! Not Peter!'

Peter was the nicest man imaginable, I'm sure he still is, but at that time he was completely unspoiled and when he fell in love he stayed that way. 'I don't know how I'm going to get through rehearsals,' he groaned.

I produced a couple of aspirins and made him drink his tea. All that day between rehearsals, run-throughs, and the time the radio show went out live in the evening, I made Peter many more cups of tea. I don't say they healed his broken heart but it did help to pour out his misery to a sympathetic listener. And I was certainly that.

From the very first day when I decided not to take the bus back to Acton but stay and clean up the kitchen at the Paris, I knew I'd found my right niche. I couldn't get up there in front of the microphone and entertain the nation, no matter how much I wanted to, but I could help the talented who could. They weren't ordinary people, they needed lots of reassurance and affection, and this I had in abundance. I knew I would never make it big in show business but the next best thing was helping and watching those who had this magic ingredient called 'star quality'.

All right, I was just an ordinary woman. I looked in the little mirror I kept on the wall; an ordinary enough, English-looking face, I supposed, but I had loads of energy. I had turned the grimy room in the Paris cinema into a kitchen that sparkled clean, and it did have an atmosphere of warmth and friendliness. I used to say, 'it looks like my mother's kitchen' and it did. But more than that I had so much admiration for the performers and musicians, the directors and the producers of the shows who broadcast from the Paris. I involved myself completely with their problems and their success and in return I found a way of life that I loved.

I didn't care what hours I worked. I could take time off when I wasn't needed. And one of the best things was the fact that when each show went on the air I was usually there in the audience applauding.

Peter Sellers was one of the many young comedians released from the services who were trying to make their way in radio. The BBC was regarded then as a training ground for young comics, and a lot of today's big names started off on the small stage of the Paris. Producer Dennis Main Wilson held auditions there to find new talent. I remember one morning when there was the usual crowd of young hopefuls. Before the auditions they would come to the hatch door of my kitchen to be served tea or coffee as they waited for their call.

There was this shy young man who carried a guitar. 'I'm so nervous,' he told me as he drank his coffee. The others had gone into the theatre.

'They say that good performers are always nervous before they go on.'

The young man laughed ruefully, 'Then I must be a genius.' He was nice looking with dark, well brushed hair and an unusually intense look in his eyes.

'Are you one of those quick patter boys?' I asked. I knew it helped to talk when you were nervous.

'That's me! Pitter-patter all the way.'

'Don't worry.' I told him. 'You'll do well. I feel it in my bones.'

He nodded his head towards the theatre entrance. 'Do you ever watch these auditions?'

'Sometimes. I'll come and watch you if you like.'

'Do that. Be my first fan.' He signed, 'First and last probably.'

When he'd gone in, I closed up the kitchen and took a seat in the back of the auditorium. A young comedian was on. Poor boy, if ever someone had made a wasted journey, he had. The harder he tried the worse it became. 'A funny thing happened to me on the way here this morning,' he was saying and the sighs that went up from the assembled producers, writers and assistants in Light Entertainment were almost audible. 'I met this Irishman, "Paddy" I said to him . . .' Suddenly, dramatically the young comedian dried up.

'Why don't you start again,' suggested the producer helpfully. After two more tries the poor boy still couldn't get to the end of his first joke. He left the stage, speechless. Another aspiring comic came on. He wasn't bad, but even I knew that he was cutting his own throat. Public standards were very important to the BBC. No one ever made jokes about the coloured races, and wogs and chinamen were absolutely out. No jokes about fellow artistes, with the laws of libel in the offing, nothing about ladies underwear, and the Royal Family must never be laughed at. This young comic managed to bag the lot. 'We'll let you know,' called out the producers, and I bet that comedian is still waiting to hear from the BBC.

'Terence Milligan,' someone shouted, and the young man with the guitar walked onto the stage. If he'd had nerves when he stood outside my kitchen drinking coffee they were gone now. The first thing that came over was how different he was. There was a bit of an anarchist about him, as if he might put his hand in his pocket, draw out a bomb and toss it among the audience. I felt the way he bulldozed the audience into full attention. And yet he didn't seem to care whether you liked him or not. Take it or leave it, he seemed to say, as if he was thumbing his nose at us. But he was funny. So funny! Everyone in the audience laughed uproariously. I found tears of mirth rolling down my cheeks. Here was a new, unusual, slightly frightening talent.

Spike Milligan, as he is known now, still calls me his first fan.

In the profession he has a reputation for sometimes being difficult. But to me Spike has always been unfailingly kind and gentle and every time I look at him I remember the shy boy with the guitar.

Spike, like so many aspiring young comedians, had begun to entertain his fellow servicemen when he was fighting in the war. Peter Sellers, Tony Hancock, Harry Secombe and Jimmy Edwards had also served in the theatres of war in North Africa, Italy and Germany and now, all returned to civilian life were working in radio, the doorway to national fame.

My job at the Paris, although officially: *Supplying refreshments to the artistes and musicians*, was that of Mother Confessor, keeper of the property of the artistes and musicians—sometimes I had dress suits hanging in the cupboard, razors in a drawer for those who'd got up too late to shave, and the odd bottle of whisky which somebody or other said he needed because of his bad cold. Musical instruments belonging to the session players, were always standing in a corner. Freddy Gardiner who used to play the saxophone in Ray Noble's orchestra asked me if he could leave his instruments with me one weekend. He was very excited because the following week he was off for the first time on a solo tour of America. I was shocked when I came in on Monday to hear that Freddy, although a young man, had collapsed suddenly and died. I felt very badly that he'd missed his wonderful American tour, but in a strange way, later on I was able to do something about it.

I was very proud of my kitchen. Miss Thackwray, the catering supervisor, had kept her promise. I had a new fridge, a cona coffee machine, a new water boiler and the shelves were lined with new china cups and saucers. Every morning on my way to the Paris I'd stop at the Lyons Tea Shop over the road to buy the bread rolls, loaves and biscuits I'd need. Once a week, Catering at the BBC sent me the rest of the provisions such as the ham and cheese I needed for sandwiches. I'd even had a new table brought in to work on.

Almost without exception, the artistes I served had worked in theatre before they came to radio, even if it had been a concert hall or a tent in a theatre of war. They were all polite, easy, nice people to work with. The slow hard grind of their profession had made them thoughtful of others. How unlike them were the television performers I met later on, who had come up the easy way and thought the world owed them a living.

The thoughtfulness and kindness of those old radio stars could really be personified in one man—the star of them all—Tommy Handley.

To know about Tommy Handley you have to have lived through the war in England. For me Tommy was part of those long evenings with the black-out curtains drawn. The blood curdling wail of the air raid sirens outside, the pounding of the anti-aircraft guns, the horrible crump and the shaking of the very foundations of our house as the bombs dropped. No one who has lived through it would deny that fear of dying or being maimed was in everyone's mind, and the intense longing for the air raid to be over, and still find oneself alive.

I remember my father would look at his watch, get up and switch on the radio. The announcer's calm, sane voice would fill the room, 'This is the BBC Home Service. It's that Man Again!' The music surged with *ITMA*'s signature tune, 'Mother's pride and joy, Mrs Handley's boy . . .' and then the warm friendly voice of Tommy Handley, 'Hello folks.'

For thirty minutes we forgot there was a holocaust going on outside.

'As Minister of Aggravation it is my duty tonight, on the umpteenth day of the war against depression to explain to you that I have seven hundred further restrictions to impose on you . . .' We all knew about restrictions and the government and the ever mounting number of ministries, but Tommy and his script writer helped us to laugh at them—at least for half an hour.

In the script Tommy was usually mixed up with some awful Ministry and there was always the plaintive cry of the charwoman Mrs Mopp as she tried to get into his office, 'Can I do you now, sir?'

Soon after I started work at the Paris I met Tommy Handley for the first time. His latest show was down for rehearsal and broadcast. He'd just come back from a trip to America and a look at American radio and there was to be a touch of America in his new series, and a new girl called Hattie Jacques was to be Sophie Tuckshop, a schoolgirl who never stopped eating.

I heard the familiar voice coming along the corridor outside my hatch and then I saw 'That man' in the flesh. He was handsome I decided, that crinkle at the corner of his eyes, the smile that came so quickly to his lips. The first thing he said was how glad he was to see me, and how happy that the cast of his show would be able to get refreshments. 'Especially me,' he said, 'I'm a milk addict. Can I have lots of glasses of milk?'

ITMA, 'It's That Man Again', the title of Tommy's series was made up of three men, Ted Kavanagh who wrote the scripts, Francis Worsley, the producer who kept it all together, and Tommy who brought the words to life. As I watched the programmes being rehearsed I realised that Tommy was no ordinary man. No one could ever call him just a radio comedian. He had style. He had magic. And the man himself had warmth, generosity and kindness. He had a great spirit.

As a treat I used to bring Brian to watch some of his shows. Tommy had no children of his own and he took a special interst in the young. He did a lot of work for Boys' Clubs. When he saw Brian wearing the uniform of the Boys' Brigade, Tommy slipped half a crown in his hand, towards his subscriptions. After that there was always half a crown for Brian.

★   ★   ★

It wasn't all sweetness and light, by any means. I had the occasional run-in with someone or other. Jimmy Edwards was a case in point. That happened much later on when he was in the long running show *Take It From Here*. It ran for eleven years and Jimmy Edwards took the part of 'Dad Glum' a dictatorial irrascible character that suited him to perfection.

I'd had a long day. There'd been a morning recording show, rehearsals for *Take It From Here* that had lasted up till the evening, and now it was to be recorded at eight-thirty. After the show which I intended to watch, the cast always went over to the pub across the road and I usually joined Miss Thackwray there.

I was ready to leave when there came a pounding on my hatchway. 'Open up,' bellowed a well-known stentorian voice, 'Open up.' There are ways and means to persuade a lady to open up her hatchway, but this wasn't one. 'Sorry, I'm closed,' I called back.

'Woman!' shouted Jimmy, 'I'm the star of this show. When I want a cup of tea I expect you to make it.'

Woman! That did it. Calling me woman! I flung up the hatchway. 'Mr Edwards,' I said frostily, 'you may be the star of the show, but I'm the star of this kitchen. And it's closed!' Down came the hatchway.

As soon as he'd gone I began to worry. I was just the girl who made the tea, and Jimmy Edwards, as he said, was the star of the show. If he wanted to be awkward and take his complaint to someone higher up, I might be in trouble.

After the show when I was in the pub with Miss Thackwray, a large figure strode over to our table. 'Here it comes,' I thought, 'Hold your tongue Rose, whatever he says.

'What are you drinking?' the bristling moustaches of Jimmy Edwards were a few inches from my face. 'Sorry about that earlier on.' He winked. I smiled, and after that we were always the best of friends.

One of the rules of the BBC was that performers should always be correctly dressed. Dinner jackets were obligatory for the announcers and when *Old Tyme Music Hall* was recorded all the music hall stars dressed in full stage regalia. There was Nellie Wallace with her fur tippet and George Robey with his bowler hat. Also Nosmo King, the veteran comedian who would always come into my kitchen for a steaming hot cup of tea and a drop of rum from the flask he carried with him.

'Go on, have a drop of rum with me, Rose,' he'd say.

I didn't like the smell, but he was such a sweet old man that I usually said yes. He told me once how he came to be called Nosmo King. 'I was trying to make my way in Music Hall,' he said, 'and getting nowhere, so I thought I'd change my name. I was on this train and I saw the sign, "No Smoking". That's it, I decided. Cut it in half and what do you have: Nosmo King!'

As I started to laugh he held out his little snuff box to me. 'That's why I had to give up smoking, but have a pinch of snuff, Rose, it's much better than those fags you smoke.'

The rum I could take, but not the snuff.

I sometimes found myself involved with the shows. Like the time on the Charlie Chester show when the actress booked to do a gag didn't turn up.

'You can do it for us, Rose,' urged Charlie. 'I'll cue you in.' He rehearsed me once, and then when the show started I sat in the stalls as a member of the audience. Suddenly on cue I sprang to my feet, marched down to the stage, pushed my way to the mike and shouted, 'What a load of old tripe! I've had enough. Put the kettle on, Ron. I'm coming home.' The audience gasped, did a double take, then applauded like mad, when they realised that I was part of the show.

When I got home that night Grace, my sister, and her husband Ronnie were waiting for me as usual. They loved to have me recount all the things that had happened during my day at the Paris.

'Didn't you hear me on the Charlie Chester, *Stand Easy Show*?' I asked them. 'That was me asking Ron to put the kettle on.'

*　　　*　　　*

Living with Grace and Ronnie had worked out perfectly. Their house was just around the corner from Petersfield Road. Grace called in to see my mother every day, and I was able to see Brian all the time. Although Grace's children, Marianne and Peter, were younger than Brian, they always took him away with them for holidays at Littlehampton in Sussex.

Ronnie was friendly with two old ladies who

owned one of the Soap Suds Island Laundries. When the Laundry closed down, the yard, which used to house a van became empty. Although he'd never done any carpentry or building in his life, Ronnie decided to build a caravan in the Laundry yard. He drew up a plan and built a splendid twenty foot long caravan. Eventually it was towed down to a Caravan Site at Littlehampton, and that's where we spent most of our holidays.

When Brian was fifteen we started talking about his future. My father wanted him to learn a trade, something that he himself had never been able to do. My father had worked hard all his life and always at the back of his mind was the thought that if he'd been apprenticed to a trade his life would have been much more affluent. He was very pleased when Napier's told him that they would accept his grandson as apprentice to a coppersmith.

'How d'you feel about it Brian?' I asked him.

Brian who at fifteen was nearly six foot tall said, 'Mum, I want to join the army.'

I couldn't believe my ears. Why in the world did he want to be a soldier?

'It's a great life,' insisted Brian, 'full of adventure. I want to join the Coldstream Guards.'

It must be the uniform that had caught his eye, I decided, the big fur busby and the smart red jacket. Fortunately he wasn't old enough to join up. He'd grow out of it I thought. By the time he was seventeen he would have changed his mind. Brian finally agreed that he would become a coppersmith's apprentice—for the time being.

After our divorce in 1947, Burt, Brian's father, had re-married. Burt worked at Napier's so he saw Brian now and then, but he made no real effort to keep up a relationship with his son. I hoped that Brian didn't miss a father's influence, but I also knew that Brian didn't want another man to take his place. As I had no plans to re-marry that didn't matter until I met Ted who was a session man at the Paris.

Music had always been an important part of my life, and now my days were often filled with music. The musicians who played at the Paris were either part of one of the big bands or session men, that is brilliant musicians who could come along and fit into an orchestra. Ted was one of these. He was a talented saxophone player.

Like most musicians, his character could be volatile, and he was sometimes moody, but he was never a boring companion.

As an audience musicians are the toughest in the world. They've heard it all, the thousands of comics, the wittiest dialogue in the business, and to break up the boys in the band and make them laugh means that the performer is really good. Spike Milligan could do this, so could

Peter Sellers and so could the rest of the crazy team who became the Goon Show.

It turned out that Ted had marriage on his mind. He wanted to settle down, buy a nice little bungalow on the coast and grow roses between sessions with his saxophone. I liked Ted very much. We were about the same age, he was good looking and generous, in fact, as far as I could see, he was ideal husband material. At least half of me, the female part that worried about growing old alone, finding money to pay the rent, and things like that, thought so. The other half, the part of me that was enjoying my job, enjoying feeling an individual, wasn't so sure.

He persuaded me to take him home and introduce him to my parents. We got off the bus and were walking down Petersfield Road. Suddenly in the distance I saw Brian, and at that same moment Brian saw us.

My son had seen me with men friends before and I'd noticed that when he did he always did an about turn and took any other direction to avoid us. I understood him. He didn't want to see his mother with any man but his father.

'Isn't that Brian?' asked Ted, who had met him when he came to the Paris.

'Yes, that's Brian.'

'Why didn't he come up and speak to us?'

'You know what funny creatures boys are. He'd run a mile rather than have to speak to his mother in the street.'

'That boy needs a father's hand,' said Ted sternly. 'It's time you married me Rose, and let me take that boy in hand.'

Everything inside me revolted that this man should calmly think he had rights on Brian. My son should make his own decisions, his own mistakes without Ted's help. No one was 'going to take that boy in hand', unless Brian wanted them to.

'Ted,' I said to him, as calmly as I could. 'I'd better tell you now. I don't want to get married. If you want our friendship to go on as it is, all right, but no more marriage talk.'

He couldn't understand me. He was offering me what he thought every woman wanted. We split up shortly afterwards because his male pride had been so affronted. The other day I met him again. He's still a session musician at the Paris and he still didn't understand. 'Why did you turn me down, Rose?' he asked. 'You could have been a lady of leisure with your own home.'

Although I used Brian as my excuse all those years ago, I guessed I'd been fooling myself. I didn't marry Ted because I enjoyed running my own life. I didn't want to be subservient to any man again even if I did miss out on the bungalow with the roses round the door.

★   ★   ★

Ted wasn't the only musician I kept company with. There was another man who, in his way, had quite an influence on my life. His name was Gerry Bright, he was from the East End of London and he never lost his accent.

Before I knew him well I was present at a funny little incident. Gerry Bright, who was known to the music world and the world of entertainment as Geraldo, was rehearsing with his orchestra.

'Mr Geraldo,' said the producer, 'let's close the programme in this way. You come up to the mike and say, "The clock on the wall says Geraldo that's all." Don't you think that would be rather a good idea?'

Geraldo smiled, brought his baton down to close the number walked up to the mike and spoke the fateful words. It was quite true he hadn't lost a syllable of his strong East End accent.

The producer hesitated, thought hard, then hesitated again. At last he said, 'Mr Geraldo—no offence of course—but wouldn't it be a good idea if you took some elocution lessons?'

'Wot!' exclaimed Geraldo indignantly, 'but I 'ave.'

Gerry was a lovely man and he was the first to laugh about the incident. He was a fine musician who had studied at the Royal

Academy of Music and in the forties and fifties the sweet music of Geraldo and his Orchestra occupied much the same position in England that Glenn Miller had once had in the States.

He was a soft-voiced, very polite man, and I always found his accent endearing. I don't think I've ever known a man who dressed so immaculately. For some reason, we hit it off from the first day. Every time Geraldo and his orchestra recorded at the Paris he'd come through the back door to have a chat with me, or asked me to sit with him during the breaks between rehearsals.

We had plenty to talk about, Gerry's second marriage had just broken up and he needed a sympathetic ear, and he also took an interest in my son. He had no children of his own and when I told him that Brian wanted to learn to play the saxophone he said, 'It takes a special kind of personality to play in an orchestra, d'you think Brian has this?'

'How d'you mean?'

'To be a good musician takes long painful hours of practice and most young boys would rather be out playing football. Is Brian really serious?'

Brian, who by now had heard some of the best bands in Britain play at the Paris, insisted that he was very serious.

Ivor Mairants who had played in Geraldo's orchestra but was now a professional teacher agreed to take Brian on as a pupil and Gerry said he would lend him a saxophone. For the first few weeks Brian was very enthusiastic but by the sixth week his spirits were flagging. Just as Gerry had told him, to be a musician takes dedication. Ivor Mairants very kindly handed me back the money for the lessons Brian didn't take and Gerry got his saxophone back.

Although my son didn't become a saxophonist my friendship with Gerry grew. One day he told me that the orchestra was going to do a tour of Scotland. 'Why don't you take some time off and come with us?' he asked.

I looked at him. I was old enough, experienced enough to know what he meant. 'Thanks Gerry,' I said. 'I'll think about it.' I did think about it, and I decided not to go. Gerry was Jewish, so marriage was out. If he married again it would certainly be to someone of the same faith. And there was something else. I had a son and when he grew up I wouldn't want him to ever find out that his mother had gone off on a holiday with a bandleader, even a bandleader as nice as Gerry.

And then something happened that took all thoughts of holidays out of my head. One morning I was about to leave for work when Brian came rushing in. 'Grandad's been taken ill at Napier's. He's in hospital. Will you go round and tell Nan.'

I hurried round to my mother. To my

amazement she didn't become agitated or panic. 'I've had this feeling that something was wrong,' she told me. While we were talking an ambulance drew up outside the little mortuary over the road. She sighed, 'Rose,' she whispered, 'that's your father they're taking in there.'

She was right. My father had suffered a stroke and died immediately. We missed him so much. His life had been filled with activity. He was such a good man, helping others whenever he could, working in Boys' Clubs, visiting old age pensioners to help massage away their arthritic pains, and being the kind of father his daughters were so proud of.

★　　　★　　　★

By 1952 television was no longer a bit of a bogey for sound radio. It was here to stay. The programmes weren't always up to much, there were quite a few breakdowns when the potter and his wheel would flash on to the screen, but a number of artistes who worked at the Paris drifted away into television.

Tommy Handley had died. His death had stunned the nation. I shall always remember the last time I saw him. It was Christmas Day and I was on duty. Christmas Day broadcasts were some of the most important of the year, but I thought I deserved a Christmas Dinner like everyone else, and I popped over to the restaurant at the Aolian Hall to have it. On my way in I bumped into Tommy Handley. He had a bottle of wine tucked under his arm.

'Come on, Rose,' he said to me, 'let's have Christmas Dinner together and drink this bottle of wine. My wife's in hospital, I'm all alone, come and cheer me up.'

His jokes cheered me up, of course. Very soon after he died suddenly. For ten years he had entered the home and the hearts of everyone in Britain. When he died the programme *ITMA* died with him. Nothing has ever been quite so good or has taken its place. I remember how Princess Elizabeth and her sister Princess Margaret came to watch his show one evening. I had never seen anyone in my life more beautiful than Princess Margaret with her wonderful gentian blue eyes. The BBC had laid on a great feast at the Paris, waitresses, butlers, and bottles and bottles of champagne. But the Princesses didn't touch a thing. They saw the show, met Tommy Handley and the rest of us, then departed. But we all enjoyed the BBC's hospitality to the hilt.

I was a great fan of Frank Sinatra and when he came to the Paris to sing on radio I was the first into his dressing room with a cup of coffee. To my delight he asked for a second cup enabling me to have a closer look at my idol. Rosemary Clooney was another Hollywood star who came and sang. I stood next to a tall, balding man who was in ecstasy while she sang. 'Isn't she wonderful?' he clutched my arm, 'Isn't she a dream?' I was quite surprised to discover that this was her husband José Ferrer. I don't think they're married any longer.

The Goon Show was now very popular. The crazy antics of Peter Sellers, Harry Secombe and Spike Milligan with their weird sound effects kept the nation laughing, but not always me.

'Rose,' said Harry Secombe to me one day, 'Have you ever made a custard tart. One of those lovely ones like my Mam in Wales used to make.'

'Well I could have a go if you like, Harry.'

'You'd be doing me a real favour, girl. It's for Spike, you see. He's been looking a bit peaky. I'd like to make him a little present.'

I took great pains with that custard tart. I stood in Grace's kitchen making pastry as light as a feather, even sprinkling a little nutmeg on the luscious custard top. Harry was very grateful. 'That's proper lovely. Just the stuff to fatten Spike up.'

The Goon Show went out live as usual. The sound effects which they borrowed from the drama department, the sheets of metal for thunder, the whistles, the rattles, trays of gravel for footsteps, even a bag of beads for the sound of someone's teeth rattling, were as usual, a riot. In the last few moments of the show Harry darted off stage and came on with something behind his back.

'Now then,' shouted Spike into the microphone, 'what's this?' A slosh! Screams of joy from the audience. 'You rotten swine. Custard!' While the audience fell apart Spike yelled, 'Scrape me off and take me home' I sat grim-faced, not at all amused. Spike blew out a jet of lovely egg custard, dashed a few crumbs of delicious flaky pastry from his hair and removed a speck of nutmeg from his nose.

I went in search of the terrible Harry. 'Rose,' moaned Spike as I pushed past him. 'To think you'd help that fiend plaster me with custard!'

Peals of wild Welsh laughter came from behind a locked door. I should have known better when a Goon asked for a custard pie.

*   *   *

Early in 1952 I received a letter from my pen friends in America, Paula and Edna Warner. Would Brian like to come out and stay with them, all expenses paid? Brian decided that he didn't want to go, so I wrote back, 'Could I come instead?' Their answer came back straight away. 'We'll book your passage whenever you want.'

I was overjoyed. I couldn't imagine anything more exciting than a holiday in America.

However, when I asked for a month's unpaid leave from the BBC, cold water was instantly dashed in my face. 'Sorry only monthly paid staff can take unpaid leave.'

'But I'm on the staff.'

'Not the right end, unfortunately.'

I felt very angry that there should be a rigid line drawn between the lowly weekly paid staff and the monthly. 'In that case,' I said, 'please take my notice to quit. I'm off to America.'

The woman who looked after these matters at the BBC stared at me unbelievingly. 'But you can't do that. You'll lose your pension rights.' Pension, what did I want with a pension? I was young enough to be sailing off to New York.

Brian said to me before I left, 'Copper's a dying trade, Mum.'

Now where had I heard those words before, I wondered. A fourteen year-old girl had said them way back in the twenties about colour photography.

'Just stay with your dying trade will you Brian, until I get back.'

All my problems could wait until I'd been to America.

CHAPTER TEN

FEELING AT HOME IN AMERICA

'I'm from Tuscaloosa,' said the little lady. 'My husband's the Mayor. Say, why don't you come down on a visit?' Here I was, barely five hours in New York and already being invited to the Deep South!

Eight days ago I'd sailed from Liverpool on *Brittanic* with my ration book, one suitcase and the twenty-five pounds which was all the Treasury allowed post-war travellers to take out of the country. On arrival in New York, Paul and Edna Warner, my American hosts, had asked a man from Cunard to look after me and take me to the station. He very kindly gave me lunch and later that afternoon escorted me to Grand Central Station.

I assured him that I would be perfectly all right until the train left for Dayton, Ohio, then I waved him goodbye and sat down on a bench. Now I felt that I'd really arrived in America. Rose Neighbour from Acton, London, sitting on a bench in Grand Central Station, a place I'd only seen before in a movie. I could have been on a film set. All I needed was Judy Garland on the back of a luggage wagon belting out, 'Chattanooga Chu-Chu,' or Alice Faye dancing down the platform singing 'I'm Alabamy Bound,' and my day would be complete.

Instead a small lady, not more than five feet tall, picked her way daintily round the suitcase at my feet, smiled at me, then sat down beside me. 'I see you're from London, England,' she said in a soft drawling voice, her eyes rested on the labels I'd pasted all over my suitcase, 'I went to London once when I was a girl.'

I was delighted to have someone to talk to, someone to help while away the time until my train left.

'It was just lovely,' she continued. 'I went riding in Rotten Row, near that beautiful Park Lane where all the aristocrats used to live.' I watched her as she spoke. She had a delicate little face with a skin as soft as a petal from a magnolia blossom. She wasn't young, well over sixty, but her hair was still dark and beautifully arranged under a smart little hat. All the women in New York seemed so exquisitely groomed they made me feel like a country bumpkin. After the dowdy clothes we wore in England—we'd been on clothes coupons for years—the women of New York were eye-catching.

We chatted together and, as is sometimes the case with complete strangers, I told her my story. I recounted how the Warners had paid my fare to Dayton, Ohio, how I'd never been out of England before and just how excited I was to be in America. She was the first American woman I'd spoken to in New York and I told her how much I liked her soft, slow drawl.

'Ah, that's because I'm from the South,' she said. 'We all talk this way, back home in Tuscaloosa, Alabama.'

'Just like Scarlet O'Hara in *Gone with the Wind*. Oh, how I loved that film.'

'Then you must see my home. It's one of the real old Southern mansions. There aren't many of them left. You tell your friends the Warners that Mrs Nichols of Tuscaloosa invites you all to come down on a visit.'

'But you don't know me?'

She leant over and patted my hand. 'I like you, that's enough and I want you to like America.'

I knew I would like America even if I hadn't met Mrs Nichols. This was more than just a holiday for me, it was a journey to the land where I should have lived if Carl hadn't been killed. But Mrs Nichols gave me the warmest welcome any one could. She and her husband were attending a convention in New York and staying at the Waldorf Astoria. She'd arranged to meet him in Grand Central Station after he'd paid a business call nearby, and when he came they both insisted that I have dinner with them before my train left.

I didn't sleep on the overnight journey to

Dayton. Not because the train wasn't comfortable but because my head was filled with thoughts of the past and the present. If I hadn't fallen in love with Carl none of this would have happened. I wouldn't have become interested in America and started my long pen friendship with the Warners. I wouldn't have sailed on the Cunard Liner from Liverpool.

I smiled to myself. That old fortune teller in the Mile End Road had been right after all. I'd remembered her as I stood on the *Brittanic* gazing down at the long wake of the ship streaming out behind us. Was this the first of the journeys she'd told me about? She'd certainly been right about meeting and working with famous people. No one could be more famous than the future Queen of England and her sister Princess Margaret who'd visited the Paris to watch Tommy Handley at work. Peter Sellers was becoming famous, too, and hadn't Frank Sinatra drunk my coffee and asked for more? Perhaps my job wasn't the kind they wrote about in the gossip columns but I certainly poured tea for the famous. Then I remembered that I'd thrown up my job. I no longer worked for the BBC. That definitely wasn't the kind of thing I wanted to think about. I'd worry about being unemployed on the ship home, not on the train outward bound.

And what a wonderful trip over it had been. My passage had cost £36, tourist class, but I'd enjoyed more luxury and better food than I'd ever had in my life. For eight days everyone on board had been treated as a very special person. I'd shared a cabin with two other women. One, middle-aged, was going out to work as Nanny to the family of politician, Tony Wedgwood Benn. She wanted to see her daughter in America and this was her way of getting her passage paid. The other woman didn't leave the cabin. She was sick all the way over. But I enjoyed every moment. The atmosphere on the ship was one of excitement and adventure. For most travellers it was their first time abroad since the war.

When morning came I looked out of the train window at America. The vastness of the landscape astonished me. Used as I was to the little patchwork fields of England, the green rolling hills, the immense pasture lands, even the size of the trees seemed enormous. 'Wait till you see America,' Carl had told me, 'it's really something.' I looked out at his land and I recognised a place where I could be happy. Without knowing why, I loved America.

The black waiter who served refreshments on the train leaned in from the aisle holding a tray on which was a small pot with one tea bag, a jug of warm water, one of cream and a cup and saucer. 'I found your tea, ma'am,' he said triumphantly. I thanked him for being so clever. Well, you can't have everything, Rose, I said to myself, but you've got a small brown tea-pot in your suitcase and who knows, you might even teach the Americans to make tea.

As the train drew into Dayton I suddenly felt a twinge of anxiety. Would the Warners like me? Whether people liked me or not had never worried me overmuch until now, but the Warners had got me as a houseguest for at least a month. We'd been corresponding for years; we weren't strangers to each other and yet, would they still like their pen-pal for twenty-four hours a day? I stepped out onto the platform feeling more nervous than I thought possible.

'Rose!' A young girl came bounding across the platform and kissed me soundly. She was dark haired and round faced and she must be Nancy, the Warner's pretty sixteen-year-old daughter. Then I saw Paul, tall with greying black hair and a wide grin and at his side Edna, sweet faced and smiling. We all embraced and talked and laughed and I knew there was nothing to worry about. From that first moment we liked each other as people.

The Warner home was a farm in Greenville an hour's ride from Dayton. The farmhouse stood in acres of corn with woodlands behind and it was more luxurious and spacious than any home I'd been in before. Timber built, the house was completely lined with what they called knotty pine. There was a huge modern kitchen filled with the kind of gadgets I'd never even read about, and in my bedroom yellow dotted Swiss curtains billowed into the warm air.

'Don't you like it?' asked Edna anxiously when she saw my bewildered expression.

'Edna,' I said, 'to begin with you've got two bathrooms and that takes some getting used to. At home in Acton when we want a bath we use a tin tub in the kitchen and the toilet is in the back-yard.'

'You mean things are different in London?'

'Different! Just wait till I tell you.' That was the beginning of the Rose Neighbour saga. The Warner family never tired of hearing about Petersfield Road and the Nestor family. I was the first Englishwoman to stay in Greenville, Ohio. I don't say I was a typical example of English womanhood. If I'd been brought up in Knightsbridge my stories would have been different, but Acton, West London, was a completely new world to the Warners and their neighbours and friends. I was a walking, talking phenomenon.

'Tell us about the bombing, Rose,' they'd say. 'The time when London caught fire.' The people in Greenville had literally been untouched by the war. They had never seen a bomb fall or felt the sick horror of watching a row of houses collapse like a deck of cards, knowing that inside those houses were men, women and children.

Many of the Greenville community came from German stock. My country, England, had just fought a war with Germany, I could have been met with some hostility, but these people were not biased; they were American first. Ruth, Edna's sister had corresponded all through the war with a German woman who lived in Berlin. She'd lost her husband in Russia and everything she owned in the bombing. Only Ruth's generosity in sending her dollars and clothes kept her going. The utter stupidity of war and killing each other senselessly came home to me once again. But to most people in Greenville, Europe was a far off unknown part of the world. They were unscarred by conflict, unworried, and to me, Greenville seemed like a quiet peaceful haven.

Paul was still headmaster at the local Junior High but he was soon to retire and become a full time farmer with his son, Paul Jnr. He used to say to me, 'Let's walk through the corn, Rose.' And the day when it had grown way above his six feet height was a proud day for him. Paul was always saying, 'Shall we take a little drive?' And Edna, Nancy and I would pile into the big Dodge car and drive about two hundred miles to visit a friend or a relative. Once we ended up in Columbus, Ohio, and we went to the local television studio to watch a *Search for Talent* programme.

I can't remember the name of the presenter of the show, but I think she was called Ruth. Between the acts she chatted with the audience inviting them now and then to sit beside her and air their views. It was terribly hot in the studio, and Ruth complained of the heat. 'If only I could be in a cool place,' she said. 'Does anyone here come from somewhere cool?'

'I do,' I called from my seat in the front row.

Ruth searched me out, 'You're not from Columbus, are you?'

'No, I'm from London, England.'

'Then you come right up here where we can see you.'

I took the next seat to hers on the platform whilst the audience applauded me as if I'd stepped out of a space ship.

'Is this your first television appearance?' asked Ruth.

'Yes, it is.'

'I don't suppose you have television back home, do you?'

I was stung into a quick retort, 'We most certainly do. We British invented it.'

'You don't say.' I could see that Ruth didn't believe a word. 'Tell me about it.'

I hoped I had my facts straight, but I was sure of one thing. A Scot named Baird had invented a type of television which we used in England.

Ruth politely accepted my story and then she

said, 'We'd love to play you a tune that will remind you of home. Tell me the title of a record you'd like us to play.'

I thought hard and I remembered the tragedy that had occurred way back at the Paris cinema when Freddy Gardiner had died just before his American tour. 'I don't think you'll have it,' I said, 'but I'd love to hear an English saxophone player, Freddy Gardiner, playing a number called "Body and Soul".'

'You want it, we'll find it,' declared Ruth, and sure enough she did.

The audience in that hot television theatre listened attentively to the inspired saxophone playing of Freddy Gardiner. He didn't need me to help him, but that American audience was thrilled, just as I was, and although unhappily we were only applauding his memory, for a short time Freddy went over big in Columbus, Ohio.

When we got home that night the telephone never stopped ringing. Even in those days television could make you an instant celebrity and now Paul and Edna were being asked, 'Bring your English visitor over to see us. Ask her if she'd like to spend a few days with us?' Invitations flooded in. If I'd have taken them up, I could have stayed in Ohio for months.

There was something else waiting for me, a letter from my Mother. She wrote, 'I thought I'd better let you know straight away that Brian has joined the army. His father signed the forms. He's in the Coldstream Guards and is doing his basic training at Caterham, in Surrey . . .'

As I read the letter I gasped audibly and Edna asked if I'd had bad news. 'Brian's joined the army,' my voice sounded as desperate as I felt, 'and he's only seventeen years old.'

'Don't worry, dear,' said Edna compassionately. 'All the wars are over.' She turned to Paul, 'Aren't they?'

'The army's a great life for a young man,' Paul tried to help.

Why had Brian done it, I asked myself? Why did my son want to go on playing war games when we had peace at last? 'If I was at home maybe I could sort things out,' I thought aloud.

'Hold it!' Paul ordered. 'You're on holiday. If the boy wants the army, you'll not stop him. Now, how about taking a little drive down to Alabama and having a visit with your friend Mrs Nichols, next weekend. I might find the time to take a few days off.'

He said it as if Alabama was just around the corner, but it took us two days to get there. On the trip every time we ate in a snack bar or restaurant I admired the swift smiling way the meals were served. Pride in good personal service comes through in America unlike England. It was the same in the motels, especially the one outside Tuscaloosa. In the

210

free and easy Warner way, we'd driven thousands of miles on the off chance that the Nichols would be at home, so we found ourselves a motel just in case.

'Tuscaloosa was the paramount chief of the Choctaws and he fought the Spanish invaders more than four hundred years ago,' Paul informed us. I was always remembering Carl's advice that my education would go on for the rest of my life and Paul, the schoolmaster, never failed me.

Tuscaloosa was a lovely town, very open to the sky. Segregation still had a firm hold on the Southern states and I noticed that there were schools for the blacks and schools for the whites. The Nichols home called 'The Oaks' was outside town we were told, and when we arrived at the lodge the gates were firmly locked until a telephone call was made to the big house.

'You certainly know how to pick your friends,' Paul laughed, as we drove about a mile up to the house. And when we saw 'The Oaks', it looked straight out of *Gone with the Wind*. There was even a coloured Mammy with a turban round her head to open the door and welcome us in with a flashing white smile. We stood in a great hall with a wide curving staircase the walls hung with sombre oil paintings, and there was Mrs Nichols, just the same as I'd remembered her but dressed in white and saying how brave we were to make the journey in all this heat.

It was the hot weather that made her say eventually, 'Now that you've seen all there is to see in Tuscaloosa, why don't you drive down to our summer house in Mobile Bay and have some sea bathing?'

The servants loaded our car up with hampers of food: cold chicken and ham, cheese and bread, pickles and cakes.

'You'll find the key under a wedge by the front door, and when you want to drive home, just put it back.'

It was this common trust in your neighbour that made me admire Americans so much. They were open-handed, open-hearted and had none of the insular suspicion that often seemed second nature to us Europeans. Mrs Nichols, who had met me for a couple of hours on Grand Central Station, showed me what a Southern welcome really meant.

The blue waters of the Gulf of Mexico and a curve of silver sands, that was Mobile Bay. A tropical greenness of foliage and giant oaks covered in trailing moss called Spanish lace. 'Look, they're like tablecloths of lace,' said young Nancy as we sat on the wooden jetty and dangled our feet in the warm water. I couldn't go swimming because I'd never learned to swim, but I did everything else. The Nichols' summer house was a long ranch type bungalow right on the sea with a little jetty where a boat was anchored. We 'rested up' as Edna said, and only walked in the cool of the late afternoon and loved every moment of our stay.

*   *   *

When we were back in Greenville again I realised that it was time to think of going home. I'd been in America for four months and although my kind hosts said, 'Don't leave just yet awhile,' I knew I must go. I walked down with Nancy to call the cows home for the last time. 'Soo cow,' I called, 'Soo cow,' and the herd ambled towards me in spite of my foreign accent. I ate the last of Edna's delicious dinners: the fried chicken and brown hash potatoes, the cinnamon rolls and the water melon pickle. And then one day in August we were back at the railroad station in Dayton. I sat with Edna while Paul and Nancy went off to see about the ticket.

'I hate to say goodbye, Edna,' I said to her.

She reached out and patted my arm. 'You're not saying goodbye.' Then she hesitated and when she spoke again something in her voice made me wonder what was wrong. 'You're not saying goodbye to Paul or Nancy, just goodbye to me.'

'Edna, what is it?'

'Can I trust you, Rose. I can't talk to my

213

family, can I talk to you?'

'Of course you can.' I had come to love this gentle little woman during the months I had stayed in her home. Love and admire her for she was a person of great worth. She'd brought up her family of three sons and a daughter splendidly. Paul the eldest ran the farm, Jack was a doctor, and Jim a vet, and pretty Nancy was going to train to be a nurse. Edna was a strength to her community, one of those women who never spared herself, a giver.

'I had an operation for cancer some time ago, remember I told you about it?' I knew that Edna had undergone major surgery some years before, but like all the family I took it for granted that she had made a complete recovery. 'Rose,' she said quietly, 'the pain's started up again, just like last time. The doctor says there are probably adhesions and I must have them removed.'

'Don't worry! It will be all right.' All the well worn platitudes meant to comfort, came to my lips. How the surgeons were so skilful, how modern science was so wonderful. And then I looked into her face and felt a chill of foreboding. She had changed even in the short time I'd been in her house. There was a hollowness around her eyes, she'd lost weight. I felt angry with myself. We'd been living with her day after day and none of us had seen what was happening before our eyes.

She sensed what was in my mind. 'I didn't want any of you to know. I don't want my family to grieve for me until the time comes. Just keep writing to Paul and Nancy for the child loves you just like you're family. I can trust you, Rose?'

'I'll keep it to myself, I promise.'

'I'm not afraid,' she said calmly. 'I've had a wonderful life. God has been very good and given me so much. I'm a lucky woman.'

When the time came for me to say goodbye there were tears in my eyes. 'Don't cry, Rose,' implored Nancy. 'We'll see you again.' Over her head I met Edna's eyes. 'They're tears of happiness,' I said, 'for all my lovely memories.'

Some time after I arrived home, Paul wrote me that Edna had had her operation, and he and Nancy were going to nurse her in her own home. She died soon afterwards.

*   *   *

I sailed home on the *Queen Elizabeth*. Before I left Greenville I wrote to my sister Grace telling her to be sure to meet me at Southampton for I had just a pound left to get me home to Acton. When I came down the gangway at Southampton I hadn't even that, I was down to threepence.

Grace and Ronnie were waiting for me. 'Well have you got America out of your system at last?' asked Grace.

I didn't tell her that far from getting it out of my system, America was now in my bloodstream and I was already wondering how long it would take me to save up the fare for my next trip.

Grace, my good, practical sister said, 'You must be looking forward to settling down again.'

'Settle down!' I cried, bursting with the energy I'd found in the New World. 'That's the trouble with all of you here in England. No, get up and go! It's this new Welfare State that's ruining you. I'm not ready to be pushed in a corner with a paper hat on my head and a jelly in my hand. I've got a lot to do.'

Grace exchanged a smile with Ronnie, 'Like getting a job, is that what you mean?'

CHAPTER ELEVEN

PUT MY PENSION IN THE POST

'I want to be a manageress,' I said firmly. I'd been home from America for a week and I was still fired with my American get up and go.

The Head of Catering gave me a harrassed look and moved the papers on top of her desk uneasily. 'But you need a Domestic Science diploma for that.'

She knew very well that I hadn't got one. 'I can do the job,' I went on doggedly, 'I've stood in for a manageress before. It isn't fair to tell me that I can't better myself because I haven't got this piece of paper, this diploma.'

The Head of the Department sighed, 'But life isn't fair, Mrs Neighbour. And the BBC have these strict rules. You must have the right qualifications for the position. I thought you understood, we want you to come back to your old job at the Paris.' She tried to placate me. 'When you're back with us you can look around and find something better.'

'Better? What do you mean? Like television?'

She smiled, pleased that I was considering her suggestion. 'Well there are lots of opportunities in television. Although, of course, we'd rather keep you in sound radio.'

I put my hands on the edge of her desk and leaned forward. It was probably strictly against BBC rules. 'All right, I'll go back to the Paris because I've always enjoyed working there. But let me tell you when I go to television it won't be to pour out the tea.'

I took the lift down to the hall of Broadcasting House still smarting. That was the trouble with the British and the BBC, they wouldn't take a chance. If you hadn't the qualifications you stayed right down at the bottom. They were too rigid, I decided, not enough American get up and go.

As I pushed my way through the swing doors the commissionaire saluted me, 'Hallo, Rose,' he said cheerfully, 'Come back to us, have you?'

The BBC asked me to go back and work at the Paris three days after I got home from America. I went back in spite of my disappointment at not being promoted as manageress because I liked the people I worked with and I enjoyed my job. But I decided that when I got the chance to better myself, I'd take it.

★   ★   ★

Brian came home on a twenty-four hour leave and I saw my son in uniform for the first time. He'd filled out, even grown a little taller and I thought he looked splendid, but the first thing he did was to change out of uniform and get back into civvies.

'How d'you like the army?' I asked him.

'Great!' Brian was never one for long mother and son conversations.

'Hope you're not off to win any more wars?'

'Mum,' he said patiently, 'I'm being trained to fight terrorists.'

'And where d'you think you'll find them?'

'You'd be surprised,' said Brian enigmatically.

We still had a bit of Empire left in those days

and I hoped he wouldn't be sent abroad just yet.

Next morning he was off early on the back of a pal's motor bike to spend a day in Clacton-on-Sea. Four of them went, two on each bike. He said goodbye to me before he left for he had to be back at the Guard's Depot in Surrey that evening, and I wouldn't be home from the Paris until after ten o'clock. I was glad that Brian was so happy in the army. He'd been right all along; he knew what he wanted.

My son had grown up, he was almost a man, tall like his father, but he hadn't inherited his character. I thanked God that Brian was not a gambler. He cared nothing for cards or horse racing. The link had been broken. Years ago I heard someone say that when you have a child you give a hostage to fortune. It's quite true. Since my son was born, a day never passes without thoughts of Brian darting into my mind and immediately I hope that all is well with him. I'm not an over maternal woman, but there it is, I want his life to be happy.

When I came home from the Paris that night the first thing I noticed was that Brian's army kit was still stacked in the kitchen. He hadn't come back from Clacton. My mother sat with her book in her lap.

'I can't help it, Rose,' she said, 'I'm worried. I hope nothing has happened to the boy. He would never be late getting back to Depot if he could help it.'

By one o'clock in the morning I was almost out of my mind with worry. I've always hated motor bikes. Why didn't I stop him going on the back of the motor bike, I asked myself?

'You couldn't have stopped him, Rose.' My mother could almost read my thoughts. 'If he's old enough to be in the army, he's old enough to make his own decisions.' Brian was more than just a grandson to my mother. He'd lived with her since he was ten years old. There was a special relationship between them, as there often is between grandmother and grandson.

The roar of a motor bike coming down the street made me rush for the front door. I saw a motor bike with a solitary rider stop outside. 'Mrs Neighbour,' I recognised the driver of the other bike that had gone to Clacton.

'What's happened?' I cried, 'Where's Brian?'

The boy got off his bike and came over. 'There was this tree in the road.'

'What tree? Where?'

'Good thing they taught Brian to fall in the army. He went straight over the tree and landed in a ditch.'

'Where is he?'

'He's in hospital, but don't worry.'

It appeared there'd been a storm the night before, a fallen tree blocked the road and the boy who was driving the bike couldn't avoid it. From his seat on the pillion Brian had been catapulted forward, but his army training had probably saved his life, for he'd learned to fall properly.

'He's terribly worried about not getting back to Depot, Mrs Neighbour,' said the boy. 'All he kept saying was would I ask you to ring his Commanding Officer. He should have been there hours ago.'

'Never mind the army,' I cried, using my anger as a safety valve for my pent up emotions. 'Is he badly hurt?'

My mother at my side said, 'Do as he says, Rose. Go down to the police station, they'll put the call through.' I got on the back of the boy's bike and he drove me round to the police station.

Brian didn't want to be admitted to military hospital, so he stayed at home with us for four weeks until the deep gash in his thigh healed. Every morning I dressed the wound before going to work. He was lucky, the driver of the bike was badly injured and finished up with a permanent limp. At least Brian's army training had saved him and he understood enough about discipline for his first thought to be about the army and his Commanding Officer.

I shall always remember the pride I felt when the Coldstream Guards was the regiment to Troop the Colour at Horse Guards Parade and Brian was in their ranks. Trooping the Colour originated in order that all ranks of the regiment should recognise their flag when it was raised at a rallying point in time of battle.

I strained my eyes trying to find Brian's face in the ranks of the guardsmen. I couldn't. They all looked the same. But I *knew* he was there as I watched the Queen present the regiment's new Colour, and massed bands played as the Ensign carried the flag in slow march along the ranks.

Afterwards he told me that he saw me, even if I didn't see him and how angry he was after the ceremony when he discovered that someone in the crowd had cut two buttons off the back of his jacket as a souvenir. He had to buy new ones out of his own pocket.

★   ★   ★

The BBC now had a new policy for recording Sunday Variety shows. It became a regular event for me to get to the Paris about nine on a Sunday morning, load up hampers with china and all the paraphernalia for making tea and coffee and cut a pile of sandwiches. Then Miss Thackwray and I would get it all into a taxi and go over to one of the West End theatres that the BBC had hired for the day: the Garrick, the Scala, or even the People's Palace in the Mile End Road. We'd set up a tea-bar under the orchestra pit by ten when the first rehearsal would start, then there'd be a lunch break, a run through of the show in the afternoon, a tea break, another run through, and finally the live recording at eight thirty in the evening.

Tony Hancock was one of the Variety stars who had his Sunday Show recorded at the Garrick Theatre. Tony always needed special attention. He'd see me and say, 'Rose, make me a pot of tea for God's sake.' Every time I saw Tony he looked under the weather for he usually had a hangover.

At first I thought that if ever a man was hell bent on destroying himself with alcohol, it was Tony Hancock, and then I realised that it was his mental depression that made him drink. His unhappiness seemed to hang around him like a cloud. He was not a friendly man, the only people I ever saw him at ease with were the two script writers Simpson and Galt, and Sid James.

And yet once Tony was working, once he stepped in front of the microphone he'd shed his frightened, withdrawn personality and shining through came this comic genius. The worries, the persecutions of the tortured man were still there in the script but now he made them outrageously funny. The audience roared with laughter at every new disaster.

One Sunday when he came over to me I could see that he was even worse than usual. It was not just a hangover, he was still under the influence of drink but he was making a tremendous effort to pull himself together.

He'd talk to me, then he'd break off, I'd turn and he was gone, I saw him standing apart, looking the picture of misery. I went over to ' him. 'Tony, go out of the theatre and walk about in the open air for a few minutes. Do some deep breathing, it might make you feel better. Then come back and I'll make you some fresh tea with aspirins.'

'D'you think that'll help, Rose? All right, I'll try.'

I watched him weave away and because I was worried that he might collapse I followed him. He got as far as the stage door, took one hesitant step outside, sniffed the air for a second then came right back in. He saw me watching him.

'It's no good, Rose,' he said dolefully, 'the air's too strong. I can't take it. Let's try a cup of tea.'

When I read that Tony had died alone and rejected in a hotel bedroom in Australia I wasn't surprised. I only hoped that this poor tortured man had found some peace at last.

*   *   *

Many Hollywood stars came over to make guest appearances on these Sunday Variety Shows. I remember I found Gregory Peck every bit as good looking off the screen as on. And our own show business people were making reputations for themselves. Among them were Max Bygraves, Dick Emery and June Whitfield.

June had taken over from Joy Nichols in *Take It From Here* and we used to chat together about the future of sound radio. By the late fifties radio actors and actresses were going over to television in droves.

'I don't think television will be such a happy place,' June said to me. 'It's much more rugged. Ah, these happy years in sound radio.'

'All good things come to an end,' I sighed. 'Even *Saturday Night Ballroom* isn't what it used to be.' And I used to enjoy my Saturday nights at the Paris so much. The seats below the stage would be moved out, the parquet flooring polished for dancing and at ten the audience for the big band that was playing would come in. I'd be standing there behind a long table spread with a white table cloth laden with drinks—strict BBC rules, non-alcoholic of course. But it was a special occasion, rather like a real party or a dance at the local Palais.

One night I stood behind my table waiting for the audience to come in and when they did I was amazed to see how young they were, and how informally dressed. One of these new skiffle groups was on the bill for this Saturday night, and when the youngsters started dancing to the beat of drums they ripped apart ten years of graceful gliding and waltzing. They danced each one on their own, and for the life of me, I couldn't understand what the devil they were doing. For me that was the day all good things came to an end in sound radio.

★   ★   ★

I knew I had to go. I couldn't get used to these prancing youths with their long hair and guitars that were becoming the big names in Light Entertainment. But I didn't want to change one tea-pot for another tea-pot, a radio tea-bar for a television tea-bar. When I saw a vacancy in the costume department at Lime Grove pinned to the Notice Board, it dawned on me what I could do. I could go to television as a dresser. Years before I'd done it in the evenings while I worked at the Leicester Square Empire during the day.

'Ah,' said the Head of Catering, when I went to tell her that I'd been accepted as a dresser at Lime Grove, 'I don't think you can do that.'

'Oh yes I can,' I said. This time I was prepared. I'd done my homework. I'd found out that I could have what the BBC called an attachment to television. After all the BBC radio and television were one and the same company.

'But that means you're only on loan to television. We could still call you back to radio after your three months' probation period.'

'You wouldn't do that, would you?'

They would! I found that out later on.

Starting at the bottom in television meant working in the basement looking after the extras. 'You've got to remember that a lot of our ladies started work here when television began,' the wardrobe master told me, 'and it takes time to become a senior dresser.'

I'd got time. There was a lot to learn in my new job; all the difference in the world from sound radio. Here in television when the programme went out live the dressers had an important role, they had to be sure that their artistes were there on cue, and that their costume changes were just as quick. Speed was one of the important ingredients in television but I'd always been quick witted and I knew I could cope. After three months I was enjoying every moment. And then I had a telephone call from the head of catering.

'Mrs Neighbour,' an apologetic little laugh, 'I'm afraid we want you to come back to us.'

'Why?' I just couldn't believe that anyone could be so unkind.

'Because we've got a brand new tea-bar for you in Langham Place.'

'I've finished with tea-bars. I'm going to stay in television.'

'Now, Mrs Neighbour,' an ominous note came into her voice, 'You're an established member of the BBC Catering Staff. You belong with us. If you refuse to come back to us . . . well!'

I could see which way the conversation was going. If I didn't go back to them, I could forget television. I could even wave goodbye to the BBC. All right, if that was what they wanted.

'I'm not coming back,' I said flatly.

'Now, Mrs Neighbour, you've been with the BBC for a long time. Don't be foolish. Think of your pension rights.'

This pension of mine. The BBC strung it round my neck like an albatross. Every time I wanted to spread my wings, up they came with the old routine: think of your pension. I made up my mind. They could stuff their pension. I wasn't ready yet to sit in a corner with a paper hat and a jelly.

I'd often wondered how it would sound and now I heard myself saying it, 'Please take a week's notice. I wish to leave.'

A cry of horror, 'But what about your pension rights?'

'Can you put them in the post?'

The contributions I had made towards my pension came to me in the form of a cheque for £60. For someone who was unemployed I felt quite rich. Such a nice sum of money, too good to save. What better way to blow my paper hat and jelly money than on a week in Paris?

*   *   *

Antoinette, Ronnie's mother, had married again and she and her husband lived in Montmartre off the Boulevard de Clichy. I'd had a long standing invitation to stay with her. My first visit to Paris was a wonderful experience. The whole atmosphere was charged with excitement for me, especially walking through the Place Pigalle at night with all the neon signs of the night clubs flashing.

'Night clubs,' said Antoinette, when I broached the subject, 'Tourist traps! Not for us.'

I longed to have a look inside one of these glamorous places, the pictures outside Chez Eve, for instance, were astounding, but by the time my last evening in Paris came round I'd given up hope. We'd had a coffee and cognac in one of the cafes and were going home pushing our way through the crowds on the Place Pigalle when I heard a shriek. 'Rosy Posy? What the hell are you doing here?' There smothered in mink and French perfume was Fay, a little blonde singer who had worked at the Paris in Light Entertainment shows.

We chatted and I met her husband Robert—she had told me before that he was something big in property, and then Fay declared, 'Come and have a drink with us. We're going to Eve.'

'You go,' ordered Antoinette. 'Amuse

yourself! I'll leave the key with the concierge.'

In no time at all we were sitting on a red plush banquette drinking champagne and watching the show. Chorus girls with nothing on above the waist did their high kicks and a lady in a similar state of undress cavorted with her pet python. This, I told myself, was certainly different to BBC Light Entertainment at the Paris cinema.

But the action really started when the show was over and the dancing began. Fay, an attractive doll-like creature with saucer blue eyes and plenty of sex appeal was asked to dance first by a tall young man and then by a very small compact man in a tight army uniform. He was so small that he was almost a midget but he wore epaulettes on his shoulders, breeches, high leather boots and to cap it all, spurs. He joined us at the table and told us that he was an officer in the Bolivian army. The tall young man also drank champagne with us, and he turned out to be a waiter in Pigalle.

Robert was a very understanding husband. He was a round, bald-headed man and smiled happily as his wife whirled in the arms of first one admirer and then the other. 'She's got a great future in television,' he told me.

I wasn't too sure about that, for Fay had a reputation at the Paris for many things, of which one was a fondness for gin. She had often asked me to mind a bottle from which she took the odd nip. By 3 am I wanted to go home but Fay insisted that we all go back to their hotel and have a nightcap.

I knew even through my champagne haze that this would be a mistake, so I waved the four of them goodbye as they were poured into a taxi and driven off.

A long time afterwards I met Fay again. She was now in television although she never made it quite as big as Robert hoped. 'Tell me what happened that night in Paris, Fay?' I asked. 'How did you get rid of those two men?'

Fay looked at me in astonishment. 'But we didn't,' she declared. 'They stayed the night. After all, French double beds are very big.'

'What about the Bolivian officer with the spurs. I hope you made him take them off.'

Fay giggled. 'You are silly, Rosy Posy.'

'Well, how did Robert take it?'

'Robert! Oh, he was quite happy, he slept in the middle.'

★   ★   ★

The first thing I did when I got back to London was to apply for a job as a dresser at Associated Television, one of the new commercial stations. While I waited for their answer I thought I might as well go down to the labour exchange and see if all these stories I'd heard about the ease with which one could pick up dole money were true. After all, I'd paid contributions for years and never had a day off for sickness.

The stories were wrong. I realised that as soon as I put a foot over the threshold of the Labour Exchange. Deep suspicion was the keynote. No shirkers, no lead-swingers! The woman who interviewed me had steely grey eyes and a jaw like Winston Churchill. She reminded me of a teacher I'd once had, the one who didn't like me and used to stand with a ruler at the ready.

'So you're a dresser in television,' she repeated. 'What kind of job is that?' I could sense the ruler hovering over my knuckles.

I explained as patiently as I could what my job involved.

'We don't have *that* kind of job here.' From the scorn in her voice I might have been a dispossed call girl. 'Have you always been a dresser?'

Foolishly I replied, 'I was once in catering.'

A gleam glowed in the steel of the woman's eyes. 'We have lots of jobs in catering.' She pulled a form towards her and started writing rapidly.

If I didn't do something quickly I should find myself back behind a tea-pot. 'I had to give up catering,' I said hastily. 'It was detrimental to my health.'

She put her pen down and stared at me. She didn't believe a word of it. 'How did it affect your health?' she enquired suspiciously.

I wasn't going down without a struggle. 'First of all,' I began, speaking slowly so as to collect my thoughts, 'I couldn't stand the steam. The kitchen used to get filled up with steam from the kettles. It got on my chest and made me cough.'

'Is that all?' She gave me a bleak smile. I wasn't going to get away with that weak excuse.

'No, I suffered with my nerves.' Let her try and get round that one. 'The cups and saucers I broke! They just slipped through my fingers.'

'We need a doctor's certificate for nerves,' she said triumphantly.

I still had the same doctor. The kind old Irishman who had been so sympathetic about Burt's nerves all those years ago. I went to see him. 'I think I've got nervous debility, doctor,' I explained, 'and then there's this cough.'

'Is it a certificate you'll be wanting, Mrs Neighbour, for those vultures down at the Labour Exchange?' He leafed through his untidy card index and found my card.

'I'm not going back to catering, that's flat.'

'There, there, don't upset yourself. Now I see from your card that you haven't had one day's sick leave in all the years you've been working. You carried on, no matter how poorly you felt.' His kind old face looked so sympathetic that I began to think what a brave little woman I was. 'And now you've got a

233

touch of bronchitis and you're rundown and nervous . . .'

I handed my doctor's certificate over and my enemy took it with bad grace. She glanced at the doctor's signature. 'About time he retired! All right, but you won't get your benefit until next week.'

On the morning I should have picked up my dole money there were two letters in the post. One was from Associated Television in Kingsway offering me a position as dresser, and the other letter was from the BBC Television studios at Lime Grove telling me that they had a vacancy for a dresser and would I like to come for an interview?

Lime Grove was only a penny bus ride from Acton so I thought I'd do the BBC first. The interview didn't materialise for the wardrobe master said, 'Oh, take your coat off, Rose, and start work we're rushed off our feet.'

Of course very shortly afterwards the question of pension rights came up. 'Will you pay back the £60 you withdrew?' I was asked.

'You must be joking,' I said. 'I've spent it in Paris.'

CHAPTER TWELVE

THERE'S NO BUSINESS LIKE TELEVISION

'If they haven't yet,' whispered Arthur, the male dresser sagely, 'it's only a matter of time.'

I stood with him, out of vision at the edge of the set, and watched the handsome young actor and the pretty young actress untangle from a passionate embrace and climb out of the bed. It was the end of the last scene. The run-through was over.

'Recording at eight,' someone called. 'Don't be late!'

I wrapped my brunette beauty into her dressing gown. She was wearing just briefs and a strapless bra, and escorted her along the passageway to the dressing room. This was in the days before full frontals and although the television camera made out that they had nothing on in bed, the Independent Television Authority insisted that they did.

Arthur and I hurried up to supper, finished eating quickly, and at seven on the dot we were back in our respective dressing rooms waiting for our artistes. They weren't there. 'Let's have a coffee in the tea-bar,' suggested Arthur, 'then we'll see them when they come in.'

Half an hour later they still hadn't arrived and we were both very worried. It was a costume drama with just the two of them in the cast, and although they finished up in bed, getting them in the period costume would take time.

'Hope they haven't eloped,' said Arthur morosely.

'Course they haven't. She's married.'

Both dressing rooms were still empty when we looked in again but this time we both heard the hammering against the bathroom door in Arthur's changing room. 'Arthur,' yelled a male voice, 'I can't move the lock. I'm locked in.'

'Quick, Rose,' ordered Arthur, 'get the house foreman and the carpenter.' But even the carpenter couldn't get the lock off. He shouted through the door to the unfortunate actor, 'If I take off the ventilator panel at the bottom of the door, do you think you could crawl through?'

A few minutes later with the panel off and the wire grill pushed back out he crawled. 'My god,' he said in relief, 'that was a near thing.'

Arthur, with no time to lose, was already trying to get him into his costume. The carpenter and the foreman said they'd look back later and mend the door.

'But what about my lady?' I cried. 'She isn't back yet. We've only ten minutes left. I'd better go and tell the director.'

The young actor's face turned red with

embarrassment. He was probably hoping to get us all out of the room first. But down he went on his hands and knees again. He poked his head through the wire and called, 'Darling! Can you crawl through now?'

Out wriggled the missing actress. Holding her thin silk dressing gown tightly round her splendid nudity, she got to her feet. 'How good of you to save us.' Her radiant smile embraced the carpenter, the house foreman, Arthur and myself. 'We were having a little chat . . . while he shaved . . . and you know how time flies.' She was, and still is, a consummate actress.

Everytime I saw that particular carpenter afterwards he gave me a knowing wink and asked, 'Any more bathroom chats behind closed doors, Rose?'

Not all my jobs were as absorbing as that one. In fact my first job when I went back to television was *Music for You*. I looked at the daily allocation sheet and saw that my name was down as assistant dresser. The star of the show was Elizabeth Schwarzkopf. I wish I could look after her, I thought to myself. She's so beautiful and she has such a golden voice. But I was the new girl, an assistant dresser. I didn't get Elizabeth Schwarzkopf who was to sing Viennese operette, I got the Ladies' Choir.

Not that I had anything against the Ladies' Choir. They, too, were attractive and had lovely voices.

'Get all the girls on the set well before their first cue,' the costume supervisor told me, 'and when their number's finished, have all their costumes on racks out of vision, and change them on the set. Have them ready in five minutes flat, not a second later.'

We had a rehearsal and then a dress run-through but that programme went out live, as they did in 1960 before the days of video-tape recording. A second's delay in changing them could mean disaster. To see those lovely, calm, queenly-looking girls trilling away on the television screen, no one would have thought that a few minutes before Rose Neighbour and another dresser were ripping off their clothes and pushing and yanking and pulling them into fresh costumes. Just like a sergeant-major I rushed along the line, adjusting collars and making sure that each one was properly buttoned up as their cue came up.

Lime Grove studios in Shepherd's Bush were the self-same studios where Peggy and I had once worked as film extras. The studios were filled with poignant memories for me of those far off days when Peggy and I had been chorus girls or extras. I remembered how we used to strain to catch the camera's eye. Now here I was dressing another generation of eager girls with their eyes fixed on the same elusive stardom.

★   ★   ★

As an assistant dresser I spent months helping the senior dressers and I was really excited when the costume supervisor told me that I had graduated to an artiste of my own at last.

'It's just a small programme,' she told me, 'part of a documentary. The artiste will bring her own costumes, but she'll need you to help her.'

As it was my first solo I wanted to ask a lot of questions but the supervisor was in a hurry. At eight o'clock that evening I went up to the small studio called the presentation suite and found it jam-packed with men standing round the set.

'Your artiste's here, Rose,' the producer's assistant called to me. 'She's in the changing room.'

I wonder who she is, I thought to myself. Judging by the crush it must be a film star. The girl sitting in the changing room turned round from the mirror as I came in. I didn't recognise her; she was certainly no film star, just a nice-looking girl wearing a Marks & Spencer trouser suit. 'My name's Rose,' I said, as I always did. 'I'm your dresser. I'm here to look after you. Would you like a cup of coffee?'

'That's a nice change,' answered the girl, 'I usually get offered a glass of champagne.'

While she sipped her coffee, I asked. 'Shall I unpack your costume, Miss . . . ?'

'Oh, Call me Gilda,' said the girl.

I opened her zipper bag and drew out first a long black silk jersey evening dress which I hung up. Then I found a black lacey bra, a waspie waist corset with suspenders attached, black nylon stockings . . .

I raised my eyes questioningly, artistes didn't usually bring a change of underwear with them.

Gilda smiled, 'Don't say I've forgotten the bikini pants. They should be there.'

They were, and then I drew out long black gloves, a red feather boa and finally something I held aloft between my fingers. A small rectangle of flesh coloured material attached to thin nylon cords.

'Ah,' said Gilda, 'that's my "G" string.'

'You're a stripper!' I'd solved the mystery.

'And I'm doing a documentary about it,' said Gilda proudly.

Gilda was full of information. While she applied her make-up which was very complicated, black kohl rimming her eyes, different coloured shadows on her lids and three pairs of false eyelashes, she told me about herself. She was happily married with three children.

'Doesn't your husband mind?' I asked incredulously.

'Mind! He couldn't be more pleased. We're buying a lovely little town house in Fulham and the money I get pays off the mortgage.'

Gilda did her act in four different strip clubs

every night.

'It's all an illusion,' she explained. 'I suggest a lot of things I don't do. Watch me carefully, my feather boa covers a lot of tricks. I never take off my "G" string and that fools the boys.'

The boys. I remembered the crowd round the set. It was my job to protect my artiste. 'Hold on for a minute,' I said, 'I'll be right back.'

The number of male spectators seemed to have increased. I pushed my way over to the producer's assistant and had a word with him. 'I'll get rid of them,' he said. He turned to the first man near him.

'You,' he demanded, 'what are you doing here?'

'I'm the props man.'

'No props in this programme. Out!'

'You! What do you want here?'

'I'm the sparks.'

'We don't need you. Out!'

As soon as he'd cleared the set I brought Gilda on. The taped music was switched on and Gilda began to gyrate. As arranged between us I took up my position just out of vision. I hadn't long to wait . . . flying through the air came the black evening dress. I caught it and then I was jumping all over the place fielding every item as it came at me. It was a very clever performance and the only things I didn't have to catch were the red feather boa and the 'G' string.

In spite of the tension of live transmission, I soon developed my own speed and my own way of working. I had to remain calm and practical for panic could be infectious, and with every show I worked on I gained more experience.

If anyone asked me the most important attribute a television dresser should possess, I'd say. 'The ability to get your artiste *there* on time.' A minute's delay, even a few seconds late on the set and you throw a whole team of people out of gear. You can't go to lunch or supper, you can't even have a quick fag, you've got to watch over your artiste like a bodyguard and make sure she's back on the set on time. If she's not all hell can break loose. The director up in his gallery goes crazy. He yells at the costume supervisor, under whom I work, 'Where is she, where is she?' And the costume supervisor goes beserk, rushes down from the gallery and dancing up and down like a cat on hot bricks waits for the culprit to appear. It happened to me on the set of the costume drama series *Mary, Queen of Scots*.

I was looking after Katherine Blake, a fine actress who was playing Mary Tudor, and she had seven changes in this particular episode. By this time I was an expert dresser, I knew exactly what to do. Each change I lined up in exact sequence on the dress rack. I had very little time to get her back to the changing room, out of each heavy costume, into another and back on the set. But I had no worries, I knew that I could do it.

We had a dress run-through before the play was transmitted live, timing each change. The costume supervisor noticed that a heavy silver cross on the last one of Mary Tudor's dresses moved about.

'Put a stitch in it, Rose, to keep it in place,' she ordered.

Before Katherine and I had supper we went back to our changing room to double-check that each costume was placed on the rack in exact sequence. Katherine was just as anxious as I that there should be no slip-ups. After supper when transmission started, all the changes went smoothly until the sixth. I hurriedly did up the hooks and eyes, settled it round her hips, then turned her to see that all was well with the front of the costume. The first thing I saw was a large silver cross.

'Oh god, wrong costume,' I gasped.

'Oh, no, Rose, no!'

I had her out of it and into the right one at breakneck speed but we were two seconds late on the set. I could see the agitated director and his crew up in the gallery. All his orders came through headphones to the crew on the studio floor and I bet he was calling me the silliest cow on earth. The costume supervisor was dancing up and down at the edge of the set.

'What happened?' she hissed.

'Later,' I whispered, 'I'll tell you later.' I knew there'd be an inquest and I should be for it. But someone else had made that mistake, not me, and I had a pretty good idea who it was.

When it was all over and Katherine and I were in the changing room the costume supervisor burst in. 'How could you, Rose, how could you . . .' she began.

I interrupted her recriminations. 'Did you come into this dressing room during the supper break.'

'Yes, I did.'

Katherine and I exchanged a look. 'You came in to see whether I'd put a stitch on the silver cross, and do you know what you did? You put the last costume back in the wrong sequence.'

The costume supervisor hesitated. 'Well I did take it down from the rack.'

Katherine, bless her heart, said, 'It certainly wasn't Rose's fault. We checked that every costume was arranged in order before we went to supper.'

The fact that I'd got a black mark from the director and crew made me angry when I knew it wasn't my fault. 'Next time,' I said to the supervisor bitterly, 'I hope that you'll trust me.'

Costume supervisors, or costume designers as they were called later on had never been dressers themselves. They hadn't graduated from the ranks and they only partially understood our problems. They were up in the gallery with the director to make sure that the costumes they had designed or helped create were properly worn. They issued detailed instructions to the dressers and they expected them to be carried out.

The head of the costume department at that time, in the sixties, was a lady called Miss Bradnock. She was one of the old school and ran her department on strict BBC lines. All the dressers, male and female were required to wear nylon overalls and rubber soled shoes. In the winter the barn-like studios could be perishingly cold, so one day I turned up wearing slacks. There was nothing in BBC regulations about keeping warm, or so I thought. Before the end of the morning I was summoned to appear before Miss Bradnock.

'Mrs Neighbour,' ordered Miss Bradnock, 'please take off those trousers.'

'But it's freezing in the studios.'

'Then I suggest you wear woollen underwear under your skirt.'

I resented that I should be treated as a schoolgirl. In fact all the dressers resented the rigid rules. Commercial television was run on much easier lines. Not for the first time I wondered if I should think of changing over.

I soon talked myself out of it. I loved my job and the BBC Lime Grove studios and the new

Television Centre at White City were just a bus ride away from my home in Petersfield Road. So I decided to put up with Miss Bradnock and prudish Auntie BBC.

As it happened, after Miss Bradnock retired, Peter Shepherd took over her job in 1967. He'd never worked in television before but when he joined the BBC costume department everything changed for the better. Now it is possible for a dresser to graduate to costume designer. He started to call senior dressers' meetings to hear what we had to say. He became involved with our problems and it was no longer, 'them and us', the management and the dressers, we became one department.

*   *   *

In 1960 when I started work in television, most of my relations were still living around Petersfield Road. I lived with my mother and Brian, Grace and Ronnie were round the corner and there were uncles and aunts everywhere. But a turning point was on the way, a time when the whole family began to move away from Acton, and in a way, the migration began because of Ronnie's godmother, the French Baroness.

Grace and Ronnie were very attached to the old lady and often took her out in the old post office van Ronnie had bought cheaply. 'She's such a good sport,' he said. 'She took us to a ball at the Dorchester the other night and didn't turn a hair when we rolled down Park Lane in my old van.'

'But you should have seen the commissionaire,' added Grace. 'He nearly died of shock when the Baroness stepped out in her tiara and mink coat.'

When the Baroness died suddenly in 1961, Ronnie and the other godson in France inherited quite a lot of money. Ronnie was in printing and enjoyed his job, and Grace liked living in Acton near her mother. They weren't going to change their way of life just because of money. However, they decided to give up their caravan at Littlehampton and buy a holiday home in Bognor. A house which might one day, become their permanent home. Other members of the family used to go down and stay there and Aunt Rose's daughter Edna and her husband bought a bungalow in Bognor too. Uncle Dick and Aunt Rose were the next ones to go down to Bognor.

Grace was always talking of her lovely sea-side house and the good clean air, and I guessed that as soon as their children had finished school, she and Ronnie would move to Bognor. I wondered how my mother would take it. Brian wouldn't be with us for ever. One day he'd get married.

'That boy knows when he's on to a good

247

thing,' said my mother. 'He won't get married. What young man of twenty-six has two women at his beck and call?'

Brian's girlfriend at that time was an attractive model called Pat. I must say I fully approved, for Pat kept me supplied with all kinds of expensive make-up. She was always getting free samples and she couldn't use it all herself. But here again my mother had the last word.

'He won't marry Pat,' she declared. 'She's too pretty and flighty. When he settles down it will be with an old-fashioned girl. He's like all the Neighbours, he'll pick a good wife and mother.'

'Like me,' I said sarcastically.

'It wasn't your fault,' said my mother, whom I could always rely on.

It was quite true Brian had inherited many characteristics from his father's family. All the Neighbour men had wanted to join the army. Burt's father had been turned down in the first World War because of a weak heart, and Burt had hated being kept at Napier's during the second world war. But Brian had done it. He'd joined the Coldstream Guards. He'd been parachuted into troubled parts of the world as part of his anti-terrorist duties. And he'd enjoyed every moment. Since he left the army he'd been working for an industrial tool firm and doing very well. Like most mothers I hoped that he'd get married one day but there was no hurry.

If Brian did get married I knew that my mother would be lonely. I worked long hours in television often not arriving home until midnight. I was wrapped up in my job. Live television like live radio was very exciting. You had to be on your toes all the time. Nothing must go wrong. Every small mishap turned into a major disaster. Like the time Sid James's dresser failed to turn up and he had to make a rapid change from one suit to another. He saw me standing at the edge of the set waiting for my artiste to come off.

'Rose,' he hissed. 'Come and get me out of these trousers.' I'd known Sid for years back in the old days when he was in the Tony Hancock Show.

'I'm not a man's dresser,' I hissed back.

'For god's sake, girl, you've been married haven't you? You've seen it before.' His voice rose. 'Come and get me out of these bloody trousers.'

And then there was my pregnant lady in Midsummer Night's Dream. Vanessa Redgrave was very tall, very easy to get on with and pregnant. At the end of the show she said to me, 'Rose, I want you to go round all the loos and pinch the paper cups.' I hoped that this wasn't a pregnant lady's prank, but when I staggered back with every paper cup I could find, I discovered that Vanessa had two crates of champagne on ice. When the unit was all together she said, 'You've all been so super, I want you to have a drink with me.'

Vanessa may be a revolutionary but her heart's certainly in the right place. She's the only lady I know who bought every member of a television unit a drink. The little people at the bottom end, like the dressers, are often left out of end of filming celebrations, but Vanessa remembered us.

*   *   *

Historical dramas like *Henry the Eighth* were becoming so popular that I wished I knew more about these exciting periods in history. Then I remembered my father had wanted to be a sports trainer and had read up about massage in books from the public library. I was in a much better position; the BBC library was very comprehensive. I could find books on any subject. Reading about these times did help my knowledge of costumes, and I realised how much these books must help the costume designers.

Costume drama also made me admire the expertise of the make-up profession. Characters in a historical series, such as Keith Michel playing Henry the Eighth, must age considerably and latex masks are often the answer. The television camera picks up every imperfection and it is no easy job to create a mask without flaws.

Ann Cotton, one of the make-up artists, became a close friend of mine. We met first when we were both working in the *Black and White Minstrel Show* that was recorded at the old Shepherd's Bush Theatre. Ann is very gifted and in time she left television for films. Now she travels all over the world with film units.

If a long make-up job was necessary I would dress my artiste first then take her down to make-up and I'd watch Ann performing her magic. Wigs are often used in television. There just isn't time to wash an actress's hair, put her under the dryer and re-set a complicated coiffure.

*   *   *

Working in television had one great advantage over radio. My pay doubled on the day I went to work at Lime Grove studios. Every extra hour I worked was paid for. At the Paris studios I'd often worked long unpaid hours just for the love of the job; television might not have been the same happy family atmosphere, but at least it paid well. I was able to save money. I even saved enough to take a holiday in America. I went back to Greenville, Ohio to stay with the

Warner family.

A few years after Edna died, Paul remarried. All the children liked Helen, Paul's new wife. They'd known her all their lives, she was the biology teacher at the High School.

Shortly after I got to know Helen, I said to Paul, 'You're a very lucky man. Helen is just as sweet and gentle as Edna was.'

Paul smiled at me. 'Every love is different. No one can take anyone else's place. I think Edna would be happy about Helen, but you're right I'm a lucky man.'

Greenville was just the same. The old town hall had been knocked down, but apart from that nothing had altered. Paul had retired from farming leaving his eldest son in charge, but he kept an acre for himself to till and hoe.

For little Nancy life had certainly changed. She was married with children and she and her husband had opened a big ice cream parlour on the edge of Dayton airport.

I'd never seen anything like it. 'It's a palace,' I exclaimed as I was taken over to the shining lunch counter. Both Nancy and her husband worked there as well as the staff. They really put their hearts into it.

'We're open sun-up to sun-down,' laughed Nancy. 'We're here with our forty-seven varieties of ice cream. Which flavour can I serve you, Rose?'

CHAPTER THIRTEEN

ON LOCATION WITH
A PACK OF WOLVES

One of the wolves got out of its cage and took a piece out of an actor; the brown bear refused to work and we had to use a dead sheep instead; and finally we were left stranded in the middle of a minefield.

'Is it always like this on location?' I asked Norman, the male dresser. He'd just borrowed my white hankerchief to tie on the end of a stick and was waving it briskly back and forth so that the British Army wouldn't shoot us.

'Baby,' said Norman out of the side of his mouth, doing his pre-war American gangster bit, 'you ain't seen nuttin' yet.'

The trouble had started in the afternoon when they sunk the Viking ship in the sea at Lulworth Cove. All those ship-wrecked Vikings coming ashore on barrels dressed in soaking bits of leather and animal skin. They had to be dried off, every one of them and given fresh costumes of Viking gear. I'd spent a couple of hours sitting on my haunches in the narrow confines of the wardrobe van sewing together those remnants of fur and leather.

When the unhappy mariners were dry and

dressed they were taken off to a new location. In the exodus the television unit forgot all about the dressers who were still collecting the wet skin costumes and packing them in hampers ready to be dried for tomorrow's filming.

'Good Lord!' exclaimed the costume supervisor. 'They've gone off without us.' In the distance we saw the BBC vans lumbering across the fields.

'That's just dandy,' said Norman, the dresser. 'Prohibited army area! Shooting range! They'll start taking pot shots at us any time now.'

The army had given the BBC permission to use Lulworth Cove for a short period of time. With the vans gone, they wouldn't even know we were still there.

Half an hour later the unit discovered we were missing and sent a strange van to recover us and our hampers. Unfortunately the driver, new to the game, took the wrong turning and there was this notice in front of us. STOP! DANGER! MINES!

'Jesus!' cried Norman, reverting to his Cockney self. 'Now they're going to bloody well blow us up'.

After a heart-stopping ten minutes an army jeep came out and led us to safety. We two women said that we were much braver than the men, but they said it was because we didn't understand about mines.

The series we were filming, *Hereward the Wake*, for television proved to be quite a rugged epic. The adventures of Hereward, a rebel Englishman famous for his resistance to William the Norman Conqueror, was being filmed around the sea-side town of Swanage in Dorset. England in the eleventh century still had dangerous wild animals abroad, so Mary Chipperfield of Chipperfield's Circus supplied the unit with livestock. That is to say she brought down Alsatian dogs who photographed just like wolves.

I've always treated Alsatian dogs with great respect and kept my distance, but they looked safe enough padlocked in their cages.

'Very intelligent dogs,' said Mary Chipperfield. They probably were, but even so they couldn't tell play-acting from real life. John Harvey, one of the actors, had to kidnap a child princess. He grabbed the small girl actress, who on cue started yelling at the top of her voice, and was just making off with her when one of the Alsatian dogs, who thought it was for real, smashed his way through the narrow bars of his cage and came bounding to the rescue. John struggled but the dog held fast. When John was removed to the hospital he needed eighteen stitches in his thigh.

The brown bear was next. He hated everything about *Hereward the Wake* and refused to join in. He wouldn't even pretend to be dead.

'I can't wait for another bear,' cried the director, who had enough problems. 'Do something!'

Norman, the versatile dresser arranged with a local farmer to have an ailing sheep slaughtered and skinned. The maggoty old hide was dyed a rich brown and then with various other aids he constructed a very life like bear. Photographed from the right angles no one could tell the difference.

Alfred Lynch, who was playing Hereward, ran into trouble when, according to the script, he went blind. An eye consultant was brought down at considerable expense from London to fit Alfie with opaque lenses to simulate blindness, but either Alfie's eyes were the wrong size, or the lenses the wrong shape, for nothing would make them stay in. So Alfie had to draw on his art and act blind.

Location work always meant lots of washing and drying. As soon as we arrived we had to find out where was the nearest laundrette and fix up an ironing board and an iron in my hotel bedroom.

Back at Television Centre there were enormous laundry rooms filled with every kind of machine; washers, tumbler dryers, boilers, dyeing vats, even warm air rooms for drying. We learned to be expert dyers as well as being handy with a needle. Costume designers often wanted a costume dyed an unusual colour. A designer would hand me some tins of dye. 'Use a bit of this one, a bit of that, and then a touch of this. If it comes out a lovely grassy green you'll know you've got it right.'

Joe Howe, one of the dressers could produce any colour the designers wanted. He had a natural talent and really should have been a costume designer himself. But with his flair for knowing exactly what to mix he had breathtaking results. I'd watch him tying up these lengths of material with string and dipping them in this dye, then painting on another dye to make a beautiful pattern. Long before tie-dying became commercial Joe was experimenting in the BBC Laundry.

We had our share of disasters, too, in the Laundry. Some of the junior dressers who lived at home with their Mums had never washed as much as a pair of knickers in their life, and they could cause havoc. In spite of the notices pinned around the walls, they'd empty a packet of Lux into a washing machine and everyone would have to wade through a sea of bubbles. One of them was unwisely given an expensive lacey wool shawl to wash. She popped it in a washing machine and it came out the size of a pocket handkerchief.

A costume designer always came on location to be sure that her precious designs weren't worn the wrong way round. On location with

Tom Brown's Schooldays we had seventy-six schoolboys to look after and each boy needed a fresh cotton shirt with a frill down the front every day. Seventy-six shirts to be washed, starched and ironed when the day's work was over.

'Why can't we put them in white nylon shirts?' I asked the costume designer desperately.

'The viewers would never stand for it,' she replied. 'They hadn't discovered nylon in those days.'

Even I knew that. But couldn't they have found something that looked like cotton and could be hung up to dry without ironing? As it was, it meant that the men dressers took all the white shirts to the laundrette then brought them back to the hotel for me to iron. Sometimes I missed out on the hotel dinner and had to ask the night porter for tea and sandwiches.

On location with *Tom Brown's Schooldays* I won my reputation as Fighting Rose Neighbour, the dresser who always goes to work on an egg. If I missed dinner the night before I was always hungry for my breakfast. On this particular occasion we were told it was an early call, the bus would pick us up at eight o'clock, so I arranged with the hotel to have breakfast at seven thirty.

I was sitting in the dining room with the

other dressers and the costume designer waiting for my bacon and eggs when in bustled the young production assistant brandishing her clip-board and acting important. 'All aboard,' she cried. 'All aboard. The bus is here.'

I didn't move from my seat. 'The call is for eight o'clock. I'm having my breakfast.'

She stopped for a moment, 'Not any more it isn't. Plans have changed. We're off now.'

'I'm still having my breakfast.'

One or two of the fainter hearts got up meekly and followed her out to sit in the bus, but the rest of the dressers sat tight and ate their bacon and eggs when they arrived. At eight o'clock we'd finished our toast and marmalade and coffee and went out to load the costume hampers with those seventy-six starched shirts, onto the bus.

I poked my head round the bus door, the young production assistant had vanished but the costume designer was sitting staring sadly out of the bus window. 'Go and have your breakfast,' I told her.

'Oh I'd better not,' she said, 'they might want to move off.'

At eight thirty nothing had happened. At nine thirty the bus driver ambled out followed by the production assistant. 'Sorry,' she said airily, 'plans have changed again. The boy who's playing Tom Brown isn't allowed to start

259

work until ten. And that goes for the others too.'

★　　　★　　　★

Dressers usually work harder than anyone else on location. They are always the first to arrive and the last to leave and it was up to us to look after ourselves for no one else would.

A television unit is a team, everyone depends on everyone else, but until the wardrobe department joined a union we had to fight for every privilege we gained. The thought of belonging to a union had always worried me a little, and I never liked the idea that the ultimate weapon was to strike, withdraw one's labour, but when we became members of the Association of Broadcasting Staff, there was no doubt that life became easier. We elected two union representatives in the Wardrobe Department, and if we had a complaint we notified them.

I first saw the power of a union when going abroad on location became an issue. Dressers worked on a rota, taking it in turns to go on location, and having a chance to go abroad with a television unit was like getting the cherry on the cake. A television series was being filmed in a Stockholm night club. The Young Generation, the dancing team of talented youngsters, were in it and every week a big name, like Shirley Bassey or Lulu, would make

260

a guest appearance. I was looking forward to my turn in the rota, but when it came my name was crossed out and Peggy, another dresser, who had been to Stockholm the week before, had her name inserted.

I was very upset. 'Peggy's been to Stockholm already,' I told the costume designer.

'Sorry,' she said, 'the producer asked for her especially.'

'Just like that?'

The designer shrugged her shoulders. 'I can't do anything. Why don't you take it up with the union?'

It hadn't occurred to me to ask the union to intervene, but I searched out the representative. She was sympathetic. 'It's nothing personal,' I explained, 'I like Peggy and she likes me. It's the principle of the thing.'

At four o'clock that afternoon I was sent for and asked if my passport was in order. I went to Stockholm, so the union was satisfied. Peggy went to Stockholm so the producer was satisfied. They didn't need us both, but to keep the two sides happy we both had to go. My life as a dresser entered a new phase where everyone got what they wanted at double the cost.

Peggy and I were good friends and we enjoyed the trip. Stockholm was a beautiful city and so very clean, as were the television studios. The programme didn't start until eleven o'clock at night and when we emerged later on in the small hours it was still as light as day.

Shirley Bassey was the star of the show. I'd worked with Shirley before. She could be very temperamental, she could blow her top, but it was always with reason. She is a true artiste, she'll do the run-through of the programme before it is recorded with as much perfection as if she is playing to a full audience. Her costumes are extravagant and daring. But I shall always remember Shirley, the dark-eyed little girl from Wales who out-stars the stars, as I saw her that night in the dressing room. Sitting quietly, her little stocking cap on her dark hair, preparing herself for the show, drawing on her energies, letting the power house inside her build up slowly for a smash hit performance.

★   ★   ★

I had an official tip-off that someone else was going to ask the union to intervene over a complaint. Two young dressers came into the Ladies walked over to the washbasins and started discussing the sacking of the girl in question, another junior dresser.

'She's not going to stand for it,' declared one young voice angrily. 'The union will soon put a stop to it.'

'It's all the fault of that Rose Neighbour.'

'Old bag!'

Behind a locked door the old bag herself pricked up her ears. I emerged and confronted the startled pair. 'To begin with,' I said frostily, 'I am not an old bag. But when I see the way you two girls feed your faces with buns you'll soon be over-stuffed bags yourselves.'

No one likes to overhear unkind remarks about themselves and I took the opportunity of telling them exactly what I thought of them. Their work was slipshod I told them and they were too fond of dashing off to watch *Top of the Pops* instead of waiting on their own set.

As I marched out of the Ladies' loo I was glad that this time I wasn't able to overhear their opinion of me. As a senior dresser responsible for the juniors who worked under me, I knew I couldn't always be popular but I didn't care for being called an old bag.

The girl they had been discussing had just finished her probationary three months. From the beginning I'd noticed that she was more interested in the glamorous side of the business, leaving the set where she was working to watch big-name entertainers perform.

Just as I thought, when I walked into the Laundry I found that an unofficial union meeting had been convened. I was just in time to hear the union representative ask the girl in question, 'What reason did they give you for dismissal?'

'They said that I didn't fit in.'

'Ah!' Everyone voiced their disapproval. The BBC phrase, 'Didn't fit in', could cover a multitude of sins, or it could just be an excuse for dismissal.

'That,' started the union representative, 'is not good enough.'

'Oh yes it is.' For the first time heads turned as I walked towards them. 'I'm the reason this girl was told that she didn't fit in. I was asked for a report on her and I gave one. I said she isn't up to the job.'

My audience were hostile, I could feel that. 'Hadn't you better explain what you mean?' demanded the union representative.

'All right, you've been a dresser, so you know what's the worst crime we can commit. She misses changes!'

'How many?'

'Three with me. Simple changes too. The last one was a pair of shoes and an apron. She wasn't on the set to give them to the artiste. She was taking a quick look at Cilla Black. I was there to cover for her, but I have my own work to do. When I'm asked for a report, I try to tell the truth. Or don't you think I should?'

I didn't like showing the girl up in front of her friends, but if you are paid to do a job you ought to do it properly. All around I saw a slow decline in standards at the BBC. The old ways of taking pride in your work were disappearing. I didn't think it was good enough to ask the union to interfere in a matter that had no right on its side. This time the girl was dismissed, but it didn't always work that way.

★   ★   ★

Working for the BBC is to a certain extent like working for the Government or the Civil Service where no one gets the sack in a hurry, but unlike the Civil Service there is the added glamour of show business with the job.

It is common knowledge that the BBC clubs are the happy hunting grounds for producers, actresses, actors and eager young secretaries. From my place behind the scenes I would watch love affairs begin, blossom and often fade away. Some of the actresses I looked after would confide in me: 'Rose, the producer's very sweet, don't you think?' A week later it would be, 'I'm afraid we've fallen for each other.'

I'd say, 'So he's going to get a divorce and marry you, is he?'

I always gave them the same advice. 'If he's married he'll probably go back to his wife in the end.' Sometimes I was wrong and the producer did get a divorce, but nine times out of ten I was right.

★   ★   ★

On location, particularly, a dresser and the

artiste she looked after could become firm friends. That was what happened between Thora Hird and myself. I'd always admired Thora, so I was very pleased when I saw on the allocation sheet that I was to look after her in the series *Meet the Wife*. When I introduced myself and brought her a cup of coffee there was instant sympathy between us.

Some actresses, alone with their dresser, feel safe enough to let the public facade of sweetness and charm slip, and go back to their main aim in life, the adoration of themselves. Thora has none of this, she isn't wrapped up in herself, she is a thoroughly nice, considerate person. And, believe me, in the acting profession this is rare.

The next time I worked with Thora Hird was on location in Barnsley, Yorkshire. She was the star of *First Lady*. Although Thora is a lass from Lancashire, Yorkshire is near enough her home county to make her remember her roots.

'Let's go and have a look around the market,' she said one afternoon when we weren't filming. On our way to the open market, one of the features of Barnsley, we passed a sweet shop, one of the old-fashioned kind with trays of home-made sweets behind a bay window.

'Just look!' Thora stopped to stare. 'Treacle toffee! Like I used to buy when I was a kiddie.'

Inside the sweet shop the woman got out her little hammer and chipped out a quarter of toffee. As she began placing each piece in a paper bag her eyes rested thoughtfully on Thora. 'I know you, don't I?' she asked. It was the half-recognition of television, full impact usually takes a few minutes.

Thora handed over the money and attempted to take the sweets, but the woman held on to the bag, 'Yes, I do know you?' Thora made another attempt to take the sweets. 'Yes of course I know you,' the woman cried triumphantly. Thora got the sweets and we were half way to the door when she cried, 'You're Mrs Longbottom's sister, aren't you?'

We worked our way through all the market stalls. Thora, like most people, is always on the look out for antiques. But all we found to buy were little china ornaments, the kind our grandmothers used to bring back from a Bank Holiday in Hastings or Blackpool. And then Thora said, 'Let's get over to the British Home Stores and have a look round. There's a tea-bar.'

'You've been filming around Barnsley for some time now,' I told her. 'Not everyone thinks you're Mrs Longbottom's sister. We'll never get out of that place alive.'

'Oh yes, we will,' declared Thora, who is a very determined lady. 'No one will recognise me.' As Thora is always immaculately dressed with never a hair out of place, I thought that unlikely.

We'd had a look round, bought two cups of tea and were having our first sip when someone shoved an old cigarette packet under our noses. 'Can I have your autograph, please.'

Old envelopes, receipts, bits of newspaper rained down upon Thora. She smiled sweetly and signed away. But I just couldn't understand what the autograph hunters were going to do with their dirty bits of paper?

We didn't get a chance to finish our tea, and we almost had to fight our way out of the store. 'If that's being famous,' I said to Thora, 'you can keep it. Someone's torn a damn great hole in my cardigan.'

*   *   *

The actresses I dressed came in all shapes and sizes. Margaret Leighton was one of the loveliest of them. She was tall and very slim, not skinny, but with an elegant boneless look. However, one of the period parts she played called for her to lift her voluminous skirts and display well rounded calves. Margaret's calves were like the rest of her, long and slim. Joe Howe, the dresser found a way to fatten them up. He constructed foam plastic calves which Margaret wore under her tights and no one could tell the difference.

Then there is Polly James, with the elfin face, a tiny little girl whom I looked after on the

Milton series. John Neville played John Milton the poet and Polly played the part of his wife who died and then Polly took on the role of his daughter.

Part of the series was filmed on location at a beautiful village near Cambridge, chosen because the old world houses looked just like those in the London of Milton's time. Joe Howe and I, the dressers, stayed at the village pub, and the lunch there was so good that very soon all the television unit were eating with us.

One of Polly's costumes, a Quaker dress, had been specially ordered from Berman's the theatrical costumiers. They sent it down the day before the scene was to be filmed. As soon as I lifted it out of its box I realised that something was very wrong. Polly is five feet tall and very slim and this dress was made for an enormous woman. I slipped it over her head and soon she was swamped in folds of material, it hung around her like a great big grey tent. Polly shrieked with laughter.

'It's all very well you laughing, my girl,' I said glumly, 'what's the director going to say when you turn up on the set tomorrow morning at eight with nothing to wear. You certainly can't wear this monstrosity.'

Joe Howe came to the rescue. After the pub was closed that evening Joe and I took over the bar. We spread the huge dress on the carpet and started to unpick the whole damned thing. We couldn't cut it as it didn't belong to the BBC, so we painstakingly had to piece it together again to fit tiny Polly. I sewed the skirt and Joe did the bodice. The landlady of the pub gave us a giant Thermos of coffee to keep us going. At four in the morning we finished it.

The men I worked with in the Wardrobe Department were unfailingly kind and helpful. Male dressers often come from the entertainment world themselves, some have been actors, we had a ballet dancer amongst us and all of them are artistic. There was a camaraderie between us, we all understood the tensions under which we worked and the constant worry we had about some star or other's temperament.

I know it is a cliché to say that real ladies and gentlemen treat the people who work for them with courtesy, but in our business we soon found out that this was true. Some of the young stars who have made a meteoric ascent to fame are often the nastiest to work with. I recall a young singing star who had climbed up with the Beatles. She was, and still is, difficult, and on this particular occasion she didn't like the colour that her satin slippers had been dyed. She flew into a tantrum and flung them at my young assistant dresser.

The young dresser came to find me. 'I'm not going back in there with that little bitch.'

Into the dressing room I marched. 'Pick up

those shoes!' I ordered. 'We don't stand such behaviour here at the BBC.' To my surprise the singer meekly did as she was told. Perhaps I reminded her of her mother back home in Liverpool.

And talking of Liverpool the Beatles weren't very popular with their dressers at the BBC either. They turned their dressing room into something like a pig-stye, cigarettes stubbed out in the carpet, empty coke bottles and paper tissues flung everywhere.

Another young singer and actress who gained notoriety with the Stones was one of the few people who managed to pinch a BBC costume. In one scene she wore a white mackintosh which in spite of my constant vigilance disappeared. A few days later I glanced at the *Evening News* and there was a picture of my lady just off to America, wearing the BBC white mackintosh.

People who snap their fingers at me are another kind I don't care for. It may be all right in Spain or the Near East when you want to summon a waiter but it doesn't go down too well at Television Centre. There was this actress who did it all the time.

'Dresser,' she called imperiously, snapping her fingers at me once more. 'Can't you hear me. I've been trying to call you for five minutes.'

I'd been studiously ignoring her finger

snapping, but this time I went over to her. 'My name isn't Fido or even Dresser,' I told her, 'it's Rose. I told you my name when I introduced myself and it's the only name I answer to. I have five changes to do for you in this play, and if you want them done please try and remember my name.'

If I was warned beforehand that I was getting a temperamental star to deal with I usually took a deep breath before I walked into the dressing room, then looking her right in the eyes I'd say, 'We've got to work together for five days. Now if you don't upset me, I won't upset you.' Sometimes it worked sometimes it didn't. Women can usually sense antipathy towards one another and it was never pleasant working with someone who couldn't stand you.

But of course there are the lovely ladies. Many of them. Women I will always remember because of the qualities which shine from their eyes. Their charm is real, their kindness is instinctive. Dame Sybil Thorndyke was one. She was a very old lady when she came to do a television reading and I was told to take good care of her. No one could have helped loving her. As the reading drew to a close the producer suggested that, out of vision, I place a shawl around her shoulders.

'Please,' begged Dame Sybil, 'don't cut Rose out of the picture.'

I told her that the last thing I wanted was to

appear on the screen, but how I appreciated her kind gesture.

★   ★   ★

Temperamental stars aren't the only ones I had to contend with. On location there were the young production assistants. Nice girls often, but some of them are inclined to throw their weight around. They have to be sweet and charming to the producer and the director but consider that the dressers don't require such diplomacy.

We had such a young lady on location with *Alice in Wonderland*, Jonathon Miller's television play. Filming was to take place in and around Hastings and the meeting place for the unit was the motel where we were booked in. By this time I owned a little Mini and I drove down to Hastings.

I had no sooner parked the car than up came the production assistant, clip-board at the ready. I don't know why but clip-boards laden with notes irritate me. I think they are rather like a dummy to a baby, the owner has to keep taking a quick look to reassure herself that she's still important.

'Ah, Mrs Neighbour,' she cried. 'You're not staying here. I've fixed you up with bed and breakfast accommodation down the road.'

Bed and breakfast can often be as nasty as it

273

sounds, so I was wary straight away. 'But the unit always stays together.'

'Not this time. The motel's full up.'

'So how many are living outside?'

She consulted her clip-board. 'Just you two, the dressers.' John the other dresser came with me in the Mini. We found our accommodation, a bungalow called 'Bide-a-wee' and met our landlady who stood with folded arms while she informed us, 'You're both in the extension upstairs. There's no electric light but you can have candles. Be careful with matches, now!'

The loft extension had been turned into two small bedrooms suitable for six-year-olds or midgets. There was a single bed and a chest of drawers in each. I knew the routine, I'd done it often enough, I pulled back the bedcover and examined the bed. Under the mattress, over the broken springs our landlady had kindly placed a cushion.

'John,' I said straightening myself up. 'Pick up your bags. We're leaving.'

Back in the comfortable four star motel the production assistant still clutched her clip-board. '"Bide-a-wee's" out.' I told her. 'I'm not spending six weeks in a loft.'

'It's no good complaining to me,' she retorted. 'Take it up with your costume designer.' I did. I told the costume designer that with all the hotels in Hastings to chose from, if the best they could find for John and

274

me was a boot cupboard in a loft, then I was off back to London.

By that time I doubt if the bridal suite at the best hotel would have suited me. I marched out, got in my car and drove straight off to London. I was so upset, however, that I took the wrong turning and found myself driving along the sea front. Frustration, anger and humiliation made me start to cry. Just because I was a dresser, I wept to myself, they think they can treat me like this. If everyone was forced to rough it on location I'd be the last to complain, but they were all living it up in luxury while I'm pushed into a boot cupboard. Now if they needed me to sit up all night altering a costume . . . ah, then I was part of the television unit, a member of the team . . .

'Rose! Rose!' Two young men appeared in front of my windscreen jumping up and down. Fortunately with the tears pouring down my cheeks I was cruising at a steady five miles per hour. I stopped the car and slid back the side window. Two young prop men poked their heads inside. 'What's the matter, duckie? Why the waterworks?'

I sniffed, blew my nose and poured it all out.

'Cheer up, Rose,' said one of them. 'You can come and live with us.' It turned out that the prop men, who always found their own lodgings, had been offered a cottage in the grounds of the large Victorian house where part of *Alice in Wonderland* was to be filmed. 'You can have the third bedroom, Rose. Peace and quiet, only the sound of birds in the morning. All home comforts. We've got it made.'

When I reported for work on the set at eight o'clock next morning the costume designer sighed. 'Location work, Rose,' she said, 'will never be the same without you.'

It was a happy six weeks filming around Hastings and Rye. We worked with a director, Jonathon Miller, who knew exactly what he was doing, which is always nice. I looked after the little girl who played Alice. She had never acted before in her life, but she was perfect in the role.

Alice in Wonderland was finished in Ealing Studios for the stars to come along and do their cameo performances. Peter Sellers was playing the King and I hadn't seen him since a chance encounter in the corridors of Television Centre. At that time he was with his wife, Britt Ekland.

I can't remember to whom he was married during the filming of *Alice*, but he was still the same good-hearted Peter. Some people change with success, their heads grow larger and their hearts grow smaller, but not him. I sat in his dressing room and we talked of the old days at the Paris cinema. He seemed just as interested in hearing what had happened to me over the years as I was to hear about his life in California.

'I must go,' I told him, 'I don't want to waste your time.'

'Talking with old friends is never a waste of time, Rose.'

'But things are different now. You've gone up in the world.'

'Ah, and so have you.'

We laughed together. 'I certainly have,' I said, 'from tea and chips I've gone to stays and zips.'

CHAPTER FOURTEEN

HAPPY CHRISTMAS TO ALL 'MY ARTISTES'

I hadn't seen Burt, my husband, for twenty years. Not that he was my husband any more, he'd been married for ages to someone else and had a ten-year-old daughter.

On this day when we met again we were both dressed in our best, flushed and excited at the special occasion. Burt pushed his way through the crowd towards me and his first words were, 'We've got a very nice son, haven't we, Rose?'

I'm glad you think so.' It was on the tip of my tongue to add, 'Pity you couldn't have found the time to see more of him,' but I didn't because today was Brian's wedding day, and I wanted everything to be as perfect for him as it had been for Burt and me all those years ago.

Burt had hardly changed. A bit heavier, perhaps, but the same good-looking, smiling man who wanted everyone to be happy. There was no antagonism left between us, but looking at him now I didn't regret our divorce. My life had been more interesting, more fulfilling without him. As we chatted, the years seemed to slip away, we skirted the present day and went back into the past.

'Why didn't you marry again, Rose?'

'I told you that I didn't intend to.'

'Didn't you meet the right man?'

'Yes I met the right man.' I still thought about Carl every day of my life. But why should I tell him that? This was my own private affair, nothing to do with him. 'It didn't work out,' I said finally.

Someone called me. Burt caught my arm as I began to move away. 'Rose, we did have our good times, didn't we?'

I saw by his eyes that he wanted me to say yes. And it was true, once we'd been young and happy and very much in love. Nothing could take that away and we had our son, Brian, to remind us of those days. I smiled up at him, 'Yes, we had our good times, Burt.'

I'm glad our last meeting was like that, for although I couldn't know it then, Burt was to die some time later and I never saw him again.

Brian's future mother-in-law had telephoned me before the wedding and said, 'What shall I do about Brian's father?'

'Invite him to the wedding, of course,' I answered, 'and invite his wife.'

Burt's wife didn't come but he brought his daughter. They were living in Basingstoke and rarely came to London. Most of my own family who were at Brian's wedding had also left Acton. Even my mother and I had left Petersfield Road.

Brian met Yvonne, the girl he was marrying today, at the wedding of my sister Grace's daughter, Marianne. My mother had always predicted that when Brian met the right girl he would settle down. Yvonne was lovely to look at, she was intelligent and well educated and a year after Brian met her they were married.

It wasn't just because Brian was leaving to get married that we decided to leave Petersfield Road. It would be more convenient to live nearer TV Centre and so avoid the long drive home late at night. I found just the right little flat at Rockley Court in Shepherd's Bush. However, in the end I moved in alone for Grace wanted my mother to go down to Bognor and live with her. Grace had a large house, she was home all day, and it seemed the best thing to do.

I was very happy in my little flat. From my third floor window I looked out on a row of lovely Victorian houses, there was a fine restaurant, Bertorelli's, down the road, and it was, in those days, another of London's villages with a real community feeling. Now in 1978, the area around Rockley Court has changed dramatically. High rise flats and tunnel like shopping arcades have turned Shepherd's Bush into a concrete jungle, unsafe for a woman to go out alone at night because of young muggers and violence. Ten years ago I could arrive home after midnight, park my little car in the deserted garage area, and go up in the lift to my flat without a fear in the world.

★   ★   ★

I remember driving home in the early hours of Christmas Day, not because I'd been out celebrating, but because an American Television show had over-run its time.

A week before Christmas I had a mysterious telephone call from a colleague, Katie Morrow, who used to work at TV Centre but had now moved to Yorkshire Television.

'Rose,' she said, 'you're taking next week off, aren't you? How d'you like to spend two days in a synagogue?'

I knew that Katie wasn't Jewish, but there was always the possibility that she might be marrying someone like Sir Charles Clore. I'd heard that Jewish weddings were grand affairs.

'Are you, by any chance, asking me to be your bridesmaid?' I wondered.

Katie laughed. 'There's an American Television Company over here. They plan on two day's rehearsal in a synagogue and two days filming in London Weekend studios. They've engaged big names: Sir John Gielgud, Sir Ralph Richardson, Simon Ward and Lyn Redgrave. I know you like Americans and the Redgrave girls, so I thought of you.'

I did have a week's holiday in the offing, but I wasn't at all sure that I wanted to work in it, however Katie talked me into it. 'You won't miss your Christmas pudding,' she assured me. 'Filming stops at five sharp on Christmas Eve. All the cast have engagements and the Americans are flying back to America on Christmas Day.'

What she didn't tell me was that the Americans were hoping to squeeze a television play that would normally take four weeks into four days. It was much cheaper to make the play in London rather than fly the stars to America.

Rehearsals started not in the synagogue as I hoped but in a large room attached to it. Through the glass doors that divided the room off I stood on tip-toe trying to see what that exotic place called a synagogue really looked like. And it wasn't as I had imagined a play about Moses or the Old Testament, it was a

281

jolly musical, a send-up of William Shakespeare and his works entitled *William*.

'The costume designer's name is Bumble,' said Tom, the male dresser I was to work with. 'What d'you make of that, eh?'

Tom was a cheerful Scot who cared nothing for the high-ups of the stage and screen. People to Tom were just people, and we were all alike. As it turned out he was the ideal person to work with, excellent at his job and unfailingly good tempered when there was chaos all around us.

As we chatted, through the doors came a lady, well over seventy I would say, certainly no longer young. An imposing lady of ample girth but with an aristocratic bearing. In her right hand she carried a stout stick and behind her trotted an entourage of minions laden with dress hampers.

'Queen Victoria has arrived,' said Tommy in an aside. But it turned out to be Bumble. Beatrice Dawson was her real name, but she was Bumble to her friends: the stars of stage and screen and the residents of Belgravia, and she became Bumble to Tommy and me whether she liked it or not. Occasionally when she was at her most aristocratic, she became Queen Victoria.

Bumble was a character in her own right. 'You ken that stick she leans on,' Tommy told me, 'it's got a great bloody big sword inside. You keep on the right side of her, Rosie lassie, or she'll spear you with it.'

Bumble was used to the kisses and darlings and smarm of the stage and screen. She was new to down-to-earth, rush-it-through television and found it hard to understand the two spiky dressers, Tommy and Rose. She'd tell us how she wanted costume changes done with a wealth of flourishes and expansive gestures.

'Canna ye be more explicit?' Tommy demanded, deliberately going Gaelic.

Bumble threw me a desperate glance. 'I see what you'd like us to do,' I tried to be helpful, 'but I can't understand how you expect us to do it.'

Bumble hailed a minion. 'I need an interpreter over here,' she called.

Tommy shook his head sadly, 'You don't need an interpreter you need a guide book. Television doesn't work this way. We're not on the boards at the National Theatre with half an hour to stuff 'em into their clothes. We'll have ten seconds flat to do the job.'

★   ★   ★

Every morning Bumble would drive her little car to the studios and park it on a double yellow line. Every night she would make her regal exit and discover that her car had been towed away and a minion would be sent off in a taxi to

283

recover it from the police pound.

'Why d'you do such a foolish thing?' asked Tommy, the canny Scot.

'I like living dangerously,' declared Bumble.

'You know what she is, don't you,' sighed Tommy, 'she's one of these Grande Dames that went out with the French Revolution.'

'No business like show business, Tommy,' I told him, 'takes all kinds.'

We really liked Bumble. She was a refreshing change after BBC costume designers and if we'd had more time to explain to her the complete impossibility of setting her plans to television, life would have been easier. As it was Tom and I were two doom-laden voices, one London and one Scottish, pleading for speed amongst the most beautifully ennunciated vowels in England.

One of the first things we had to break to the cast, and to Bumble, was the fact that all costume changes would take place on the set. 'Anyone who's shy,' called Tom, 'just close their eyes and think of England.' A winding circular staircase led from the changing rooms upstairs down to the set, and the thought of Sir John Gielgud in his heavy Shakespearian trappings missing a step and breaking his very expensive neck made our blood run cold. Then there was a young pop star called Paul Jones, who although spritely, had to wear a suit of armour and couldn't move a step unless we half carried him.

Mr and Mrs Cohen who owned Television International, the American company who had put up the money, were very charming, completely organised and experienced in making films, but about television they were almost babes in arms. In fact hardly anyone knew about television. The anguished voice of Ian the director cried, 'There are only three people in this bloody studio who understand television and that's the two dressers and me.'

'How about another take?' Mr Cohen would suggest.

'There's no time for re-takes,' groaned the director. 'All we've got left is tomorrow.'

Even though we were making *William* the American way, non-stop, there still wasn't enough time. Upstairs in the wardrobe room a large trestle table was erected, laden with food and drink. There were no English tea-breaks, no cosy lunches, when anyone was at the point of exhaustion they would crawl upstairs, grab something to eat and drink and crawl downstairs again. There was food galore, drink galore, but hardly any time to partake of it.

The unions would have gone into shock if they had seen how their members worked just to get finished by Christmas. Union rule books were trampled underfoot, and no one had ever heard of unsocial hours.

'Our artistes' were darlings, every one of

them. Sir John Gielgud on the point of an oration developed a tickle in his throat. 'Tom, dear boy,' he whispered, 'have you a pastille?'

Tom hadn't, but I produced a Victory V Gum from my pocket. Victory V Gums are guaranteed to blow the patient's head straight off his shoulders. They are invaluable for a head cold. As far as a tickle is concerned, I wasn't too sure, but this, after all, was an emergency. Sir John took the gum, 'Thank you, my dear.'

He popped the gum into his mouth, sucked for a second and then I watched his cheeks go from pink to rosy red. He removed the gum and panted for air. 'A trifle strong, my dear,' he gasped, 'a trifle strong.'

'Trust you,' hissed Tom, when Sir John was out of earshot. 'The best bloody voice in England and you bloody well try and ruin it.'

Lyn Redgrave and Simon Ward sang a song called 'Brush up your Shakespeare'; Sir Ralph Richardson read from the Bard, and young Paul Jones put a little pop into Merrie Englande. At five o'clock on Christmas Eve it looked as if we should still be there for the New Year.

'I have a dinner engagement,' Sir John whispered plaintively.

'I have to drive down to Sussex and fill the children's stockings,' whispered Simon Ward.

'And my Mum's waiting for me in Bognor,' I added.

'No one is going any bloody where, so shut

up,' yelled the director.

At five minutes past midnight we finished *William*. The Cohens caught their plane, Sir John missed his dinner engagement. I didn't get down to Bognor until Christmas Day, but we all agreed that *William* was an experience we wouldn't have missed. Bumble even asked Tommy whether he'd like to leave that rat-race called television and join the real world of films.

*   *   *

A large section of the third floor at TV Centre is devoted to wardrobe and costume. The walls are lined with cupboards, there are row upon row of dress racks where each costume hangs tidily in its plastic cover. At the BBC costumes are used over and over again; refurbished and re-fitted, this policy works very well for period dresses. Even modern clothes are altered time and time again to suit a drama or a television spectacular. There is a team of very expert seamstresses, embroiderers and tailors. Nothing is ever sold to the artistes. If an actress falls in love with the dress she has worn, she is never allowed to buy it.

The big stars wear the most expensive dresses. Petula Clark for instance has the most beautiful dresses created especially for her. One of these was of pure silk chiffon that fell in soft folds of peach from a yoke and neckline embroidered with crystal beads. As I did up the tiny hooks and eyes at the back of the dress for the run-through, Petula found the neckline just a fraction tight. Petula is the easiest of girls and never wants to cause trouble. 'Leave the top hook and eye undone, Rose,' she suggested. 'No one will notice.'

Someone did, however. The eagle eyes of the costume designer up in the gallery with the production team spotted the omission. She had designed the dress and was there to make sure that her creation was perfect. After the run-through she came hurrying down to me. 'If the neckline's too tight,' she exploded, 'you alter it, you don't leave the hooks undone.'

'Alter that dress?' I couldn't believe my ears. It had taken the seamstresses an age to fit and sew that beautiful gown.

The costume designer's voice was hostile. 'You know how to sew, don't you? Get out your scissors and get the shoulder line lifted,' she ordered.

'I wouldn't touch a dress like that. I could ruin it.'

Without another word the costume designer marched over to the telephone and called the wardrobe department. 'Mrs Neighbour, who should know better, tells me that she can't do a simple alteration.'

I shot over to her side. 'Correction, please. Tell them that Mrs Neighbour won't do the alteration because she has too much sense.'

We stood glaring at each other and waited for an alteration hand to come down to the set. 'Glad you didn't touch it, Rose,' she told me when she arrived, 'the dress is cut on the cross and we had the devil of a job getting that neckline right.'

The costume designer wasn't at all pleased at my smug know-all smile. I could see from the poisonous look she gave me that she'd find some way to get her own back. I'd proved her wrong but she'd make me pay for it. She was a nervous, highly-strung woman who was easily scared. 'It's Halloween, tonight,' I told her.

'What about it?' she snapped.

'Haven't you heard?' I caught the eye of my junior dresser and winked. 'Tonight's the night I get on my broomstick.'

To my astonishment instead of taking it for what it was, a joke, she backed away from me. 'You mean you're a witch!' She actually sounded frightened.

'Anyone who crosses me gets the treatment tonight.' I made a few hissing sounds to complete the picture.

'Don't you dare!' her voice began to rise. 'Don't you dare try anything on me!'

The junior dresser could hold out no longer, she shook with laughter. She even cackled, 'Shall I let your black cat out now, Rose?'

The costume designer hesitated not quite

sure how to take it. She gazed at me and I pulled a few Lon Chaney faces to cheer her up.

'I'm warning you,' she screeched, 'I'm warning you,' and she fled.

★   ★   ★

No one had called me a witch before but a lot of the girls in wardrobe said I was psychic when I predicted how their romances would end. Through my work, I suppose that I have developed a strong sense that either attracts me to people or warns me about them. Some people have a positive aura around them that I can sense. Judy Dench, the actress, has it in abundance, an aura of happiness and good will.

Sometimes I feel that I can predict what is going to happen to someone. John Ammond, for instance, was a sound effects boy at the old Paris studio when I first met him. Although all he did then was to open and shut doors and clatter a few coconut shells, I felt instinctively that he'd do well. He is now an executive producer at TV Centre and has become the man with the golden touch. His shows, like the Morecambe and Wise, and the Val Doonican, get the highest ratings, but he still remains the same nice person he was at the beginning.

I still meet many people I first met at the Paris. Manny Winters was a session man there, he played a beautiful clarinet. We first started to chat together after my father died, and Manny who lived with his father and mother was a sympathetic listener. Our friendship has gone on over the years. Whenever we see each other at the studios we tell each other about our families, our old parents. But we never talk about our life outside the studios, our friendship is just bound up with our work. We have never met outside the studios, never telephoned each other, and yet these conversations have warmed our lives.

There was always something happening at the Paris. Some of these incidents were so silly that I don't know why I remember them. One day a man came running down the corridor towards my tea-bar. He was out of breath and panting.

'Is he?' he cried, 'Is he?'

I leaned towards him, full of concern. 'Is he what?'

'Is he lost?'

This was getting us nowhere fast. 'Who's lost?'

'My brother, Izzy.'

So Izzy was lost. And then I caught on. He was asking about Izzy Loss. And there was only one man called Loss coming to the studios that morning. Joe Loss, the bandleader. Joe Loss's brother just couldn't understand why I couldn't stop laughing.

Television has never made me laugh as much as radio. It's a more serious business with worries about ratings and viewing figures, but there's still a romantic side to it. The first series of *The Generation Game* had enough romance in it to change quite a few lives.

Bruce Forsyth was to be the star of *The Generation Game*. No one knew whether it would be a success or not, but Bruce had an immense talent. He had just sang and danced and joked his way to fame in the *Sunday Night at the London Palladium*. The producer of this new show suggested that as it was to be an audience participation programme, a beautiful young hostess should be engaged, but the girl must have more than just looks, she'd need a warm soothing personality to calm down the terrified contestants.

Bruce said that he'd met such a girl when she was a fellow judge at a Lovely Legs contest. The producer saw her and thought she was exactly right, and when I met her for the first time in the dressing room I could see what they meant. Anthea Redfern was outstandingly beautiful. However, she'd never appeared on television before and when we were alone together she told me that she was petrified with nerves. 'I'm supposed to lead these poor people up to Bruce and my knees will be knocking together so hard that I'll never make it.'

'Come on, Anthea,' I said to her. 'This is what you do. Just before you walk onto the set, take a few deep breaths, then hold your head